Lizzy
&
the Light Below

by Jacqueline Thomas

Illustrated by Janet Learmonth

Third Edition

Arms of Venus Press
Austin, Texas

ISBN-13: 978-0-615-92689-6 (Custom)
ISBN-10: 0-615-92689-4
Library of Congress Catalog Number: 2013922251

Dedicated to Changing Girls everywhere . . .

and to the Changing Girl in everyone.

Foreword

Lizzy and the Light Below is a story for mothers to share with their daughters, about the hidden cultural significance of menstruation. Ideal for girls who have just begun menstruating, or who are approaching menarche, *Lizzy's* message goes beyond the valid and valuable assurances we give to girls that menstruation is natural, a sign of good reproductive health and, therefore, nothing to be ashamed of. It anticipates the cultural silence surrounding menses that girls "hear" after getting this initial encouragement—a silence that "expresses" a surprisingly entrenched collective taboo. It also counters the prevalent messages girls get that menstruation is merely a grooming problem to solve or a medical condition to regulate with pharmaceutical products.

Instead, *Lizzy* conveys the ample evidence I found in my doctoral research that, because menstruation helped the earliest humans understand the "numbered" and cyclic nature of reality, it is a foundation of human thought and cultural activity—something that, in fact, we as women should be proud of. As a story of a girl making an unexpected and enlightening underworld journey on the day she gets her first period, *Lizzy's* narrative structure mimics that of the world's oldest hero myth, *The Descent of Inanna*. (It also briefly retells the tale.) This ancient Sumerian myth relates the daring and rewarding confrontation that Inanna, Queen of Heaven and Earth, has with Ereshkigal, Queen of the Underworld—characters who can be read as representing the two sides of the ovulatory/menstrual cycle. Assuming that this somatic interpretation captures the Sumerian people's inheritance of a prehistoric view of menstruation as a key to understanding the universe, I have used *Inanna* to revive a timeless message of menstruation's gift of deep wisdom about the cyclic nature not only of our bodies, but also of our relationships and our creativity.

Initially written as a read-aloud tool for mothers to use to bond with their daughters at an important moment in their lives—a moment at which their self-esteem as young women is threatened by a virtually universal prejudice—it can also be given to a girl to read by herself. I have included in this volume a preface on the scholarly work that underlies the story. Reading this researched preface is not necessary for understanding or benefiting from the story; and I hope my readers will benefit much from it.

Jacqueline K. Thomas, Ph.D.

Contents

Preface

I, the woman who circles the land—tell me where is my house,
Tell me where is the city in which I may live . . .

Sumerian cuneiform fragment BM 96679

Even before a girl has her first menstrual period, the hushed euphemisms she hears used for it and the embarrassed silences she perceives surrounding it convey to her that, once a month every month, she will become a sort of cultural exile. That is, for about half of her life, she will go through an experience that, in spite of recent efforts to normalize it, is still shrouded in shame. In recent decades, women's advocates have done much good work to de-stigmatize menstruation, in large part by framing it within a secular view of it as natural and as an indicator of good health and fertility. And, while this naturalistic approach is valuable insofar as it counters the superstition, misinformation, and prejudices that have been attached to it for millennia, by definition, its emphasis on it as a normal bodily function does not consider or reconsider the relationship of menstruation to culture.

In this book, I have worked to distill into a simple narrative my study of how the mythic iconography of the world's love goddesses bears out recent anthropological theories of menstruation as a culture-originating force. I have written this story so that it can be read out loud to a girl approaching or experiencing her first menses, or simply given to her. In it, I go beyond retelling the first hero myth—the story of the self-sacrificing descent of the Sumerian goddess Inanna into the underworld—to make connections between the narrative binary of upper-world and underworld, and the larger cultural implications of this two-sided narrative structure. For instance, if we consider that women were the likely makers of what scholars assume to be the moon calendars found at Paleolithic archeological sites, we could reasonably entertain the idea that women were the first to develop mathematical ideas. Seen in this context, the etymology of the word "mathematics"—"mother wisdom"—makes more sense. More importantly, such a connection could give girls a sense of having a birthright to mathematical knowledge.

To allow girls to grasp the significance of menstruation in an experiential way, I have taken the approach of writing a story of girl who "accidentally" descends into a friendly underworld on the day of her first menses, and begins to understand and take pride in the powers that come with it. In this way, the story mirrors the female characters of myth and legend that I have studied—Inanna, the Greek Aphrodite, and the swan maidens that travel back and forth from the otherworld to the ordinary world in the fairy tales of nearly every culture on Earth. These myths and stories all contain images, characters, and narrative patterns that, I argue, track with an evolutionary-cultural "logic" of menstruation asserted independently by anthropologists Chris Knight and Annette Weiner. This logic organizes mythic story-worlds into upper and lower realms, periodically separates groups of women from men, gives women the power to weave magical clothes, and either gives them the agency to rhythmically come and go from "normal" life, or has them lament the loss of this agency. The perspectives of other scholars, such as Paul Friedrich on the origins of Aphrodite, Diane Wolkstein, Samuel Noah Kramer, and Betty De Shong Meador on the significance of Inanna in ancient Sumer, Mircea Eliade on puberty rites among aboriginal peoples, Sylvia Brinton Perera on the descent myth's psychological significance for women, and Judy Grahn on menstruation as a central cultural source for ancient peoples, all complement these basic anthropological theories.

In *The Meaning of Aphrodite*, anthropologist, Paul Friedrich lists an array of goddesses from several cultural traditions and historical periods, all of whom he counts as either proto-Aphrodites or, as he puts it, "faded" Aphrodites. According to Friedrich, the proto-Aphrodites include not only the Sumerian Inanna, but also the Akkadian Ishtars and the Levantine Astartes, the Indo-European dawn goddess, Ushas, the Greek and Latin dawn divinities, the Baltic sun maiden, and the Proto-IndoEuropean water nymphs (Friedrich 12-54).

Inanna's, Ishtar's, and Astarte's symbolic associations include the following: a stylized rosette (Wolkstein and Kramer 184); the apple and apple tree (12); a snake, dragon, or dove (this aspect is often shown by the goddess herself having wings); fine, alluring clothing; the planet Venus and its mythicized connections to the Sun, Moon, and dawn (Inanna was both moon-daughter and sun-sister); provenance from liminal waterways—often on a boat (19); beauty, sexual pleasure, love, war, death, the arts of civilization, and the fertility of the earth (Friedrich 12-23). Aside from Aphrodite's lack of astral associations, her symbols and associations are virtually identical to those of Inanna/Ishtar/Astarte (14, 19, 22).

And while Greek Aphrodite does not have the astral associations of these Near Eastern goddesses or those of the Indo-European, Greek, and Roman dawn divinities, she is always described as golden (77-79). She also shares their reputation for wearing fine robes and veils, having beautiful hair, ensuring health and fertility, and safeguarding the divine order with cosmetic ritual (Guirand 332, Friedrich 36-43). Moreover, Aphrodite's and Inanna's world-benefiting emergence from water seems reflected in the Vedic image of the Indic dawn goddess Ushas' daily appearance, "like a girl from her bath . . . 'conscious of her body like a beauty. . . '" (Friedrich 37) And, the mythos of the Baltic Sun Maiden, Saule, shares in many of these goddesses' attributes, being attended by Venus and having daughters who were sunlike rays of light, (Ushas was often seen as a group of dawn maidens, and Aphrodite was often attended by the Hours or the Graces). Like Inanna/Ishtar/Astarte and Aphrodite, Saule is related to the sea and daily "descends into her apple garden or sinks like an apple or a boat below the horizon of the sea" (Friedrich 35-36)

Surprisingly, the dawn deities, like Inanna, are related to death insofar as their appearance every morning heralds the passing days of mortals' lives (39). Paradoxically though—and yet, unsurprisingly—since they die with the sun every evening and then reemerge every morning from a liminal otherworld beyond the horizon, they are also rebirth deities. Inanna was understood as just such a cycling, undying deity because her association with Venus—the planet that attended both the sun and the moon—made her present to the world, night and day (Brinton Perrera 13). Her epithet "mountain born" refers to her rise over the mountains to the east of Sumer, a fact of nature mythologized as her lineage from the first-generation gods, An (Sky) and Ki (Earth), who coupled on the cosmic mountain—a sort of liminal island that emerged from the primal sea (Meador 15-16). (This mystical connection to an island is echoed in Aphrodite's heaven-descended, foam-borne arrival on Cyprus.) In another story, Inanna descends by boat into an underworld waterway and returns to her city, bringing back both a flood and the arts of civilization. And of course, the mythic deaths of these goddesses' male consorts, Dumuzi and Adonis reflect their death valence.

Friedrich also notes parallels between the death-rebirth mythos of Persephone and that of Aphrodite, particularly because of their shared, obsessive love for Adonis and because they both have crone aspects, Persephone's being the moon hag Hecate and Aphrodite's being the old wool-comber she disguises herself as in Homer's Iliad (Guirand 165-166, Friedrich 153, 59). I would add that Persephone's Aphrodisian iconography extends to her association with fruits and flowers, with an underworld waterway, the bloody River Styx, and with birds in the form of the Sirens, the bird-women who conducted the souls of the dead to her realm (Guirand 147-148).

The Vedic poets, the Akkadian poet Enheduanna (the first known poet in all of human history), and the early Greeks exalted Ushas, Inanna, and Aphrodite respectively. In the Vedas, Ushas is sometimes referred to as "mother . . . of all the gods" (Friedrich 39), and Enheduanna exalts Inanna over her great-grandfather, An. In one of her poems, An takes sides in an attack on Inanna and loses to the valiant heroine goddess (De Shong Meador 108). And, while the Homeric Greeks did not exalt Aphrodite, Friedrich argues that her archaic omnipotence is present in the Homeric epics since, by instilling desire in Paris and Helen, she was the first cause of the Trojan War (Friedrich 59-61). Her appellations, *Pandemos*, which means "of all the people" and *Urania*, which means "heavenly," both also seem to point to her former universal standing.

Most striking about the main elements of the Aphrodite-type goddess is their virtual identity with those of many aboriginal initiation rites. In Mircea Eliade's survey of tribal initiation rites worldwide, he found a nearly universal reenactment by the initiate of the death and rebirth of a god. This ritual death and renewal includes the following: the initiates' separation from normal life (Eliade 7-8); the initiate's seclusion in a sacred, other-worldly precinct, often in dark silence (4-5, 9, 35-37,41-43, 63); the ritual bathing and cosmetic decoration of the initiate (67, 72, 85, 116); and the unclothing and re-clothing of the initiate in sacred cloth, furs, skins, or woven leaves (8, 9, 37).

Other sources cite bathing traditions for girls at menarche. An early twentieth-century ethnography reports that menstruating women among the Yurok Indians of California took a purificatory, luck-enhancing bath in a river (Buckley and Gottlieb 194). A modern Yurok informant tells of women gathering firewood on the shores of a sacred "moon-time" pond on a nearby mountain to heat this bath water (190). Another Yurok woman proudly called menstruating women "flowers," a metaphor found in folk beliefs worldwide and shared by the Beng of the Ivory Coast who liken menstruation to the flowering stage of a fruit-bearing tree (194, 58, 74, Grahn 230-234). The Temne of Sierra Leone, equate water with darkness and spiritual obscurity, and see initiates as existing in a land of water (Buckley and Gottlieb 224). For them, the East is the place of beginnings, birth, ancestors, and initiations, and is associated with menstruation and the new moon; one way they say "to menstruate" is to say "to be in the East" (224-225). In spite of the great importance of the menstrual initiations for Temne girls, the labial scarification and/or clitorectomy that attends it is testament to the culture's felt need to limit the sexuality that is implicit to girls' coming of age.

The apparent need to ritually and/or actually limit women's capacity for a positive stance toward the sexual maturity that comes at female puberty seems related to the negative, fearful perceptions of menstruation now perpetuated in the nearly universal taboo on it. In spite of much evidence in the archeological and ethnographic records of positive attitudes and culturally significant rituals around menstruation—in prehistory, in the historical past, and in the present—most anthropologists and other theorists on humanity's cultural origins have traditionally only seen menstruation in either the negative terms that apply today or, at best, in terms of its significance for girls' physical health and reproductive capacity. Indeed, this impulse seems to be operating in Eliade's assessment of the difference between girls' and boys' initiation rites.

Eliade stresses that even though the initiations of boys and girls share common elements, "unlike, [girls], [boys] during their period of initiatory training are made conscious of 'invisible' [cultural] realities and learn a sacred history that is not evident; i.e., is not given in immediate experience" (Eliade 47). By immediate experience he means menstruation, and he says of girls' initiations that, because girls enter puberty by virtue of their menarche, their initiations are necessarily "natural" (47) and involve merely a recognition and celebration of their biological responsibilities as "creatresses" (42). He downplays the ritualized significance of the spinning and weaving that the girls are taught during menarche ceremonies and seems, like most anthropologists of his time, to be unaware of what Annette Weiner has found to be the central importance of woman-produced cloth to all human ritual, economic exchange, and expression of cultural identity. While he acknowledges an occult dimension of the aboriginal likening of girls' initiatory spinning to the moon's "spinning [of] Time and [tribal] Destiny," this "revelation of women's sacrality" does not register to him as an invisible, cultural reality learned by the girls while producing mystically charged cultural artifacts (45-46).

Women's sacrality, then, to Eliade consists only in the "springs of life and fertility" (46). He maintains this view in the face of the widespread circumcision and subincision ceremonies whereby men in cultures worldwide mimic women's menstruation, even when some of his informants relate etiological myths of these rites that tell of the first men stealing the first women's magical moon powers (29-30). Ultimately, he considers boys' initiatory rites to be "one of the most spiritual phenomena in the history of humanity" and adds that through these rites "men attain the status of human beings" and that, before initiation, "they do not yet fully share in the human condition" (3). Presumably, then, for Eliade, since girls do not receive the "human-making" transmissions that boys receive—even though the men sometimes admit that these have been stolen from now-extinct women's mysteries—women are always something less than fully human.

Chris Knight documents a similar instance of male informants in aboriginal Australia admitting to their forefathers' cooption of women's ritual blood power for men's exclusive use in so-called "male menstruation" rites (Knight 40-43). Knight argues that all initiation rites are, in fact, based on menstrual seclusion rites. He argues that the seclusion rituals that appear in most initiation ceremonies are modeled on the menstrual seclusion rites developed by the earliest modern humans (women) who inhabited the East African Rift 90,000-45,000 years ago. He theorizes that when these earliest women were pushed into close proximity to each other alongside the waters of this part of Africa during the Pleistocene drought, their menstruation became synchronized. The resulting synchronization of their ovulation would have made it difficult for alpha males to continue their primate habit of policing each one of them to keep less dominant males away from them for sex. Knight proposes that women took advantage of this change and collectively instituted a menstrual sex strike, the breaking of which required hunted meat from the men. He maintains that this sex strike—the first political and, therefore, the first human act—was effected by women ritually congregating with their mothers and sisters in seclusion from men during the synchronized perimenstruum. This, he says, led to a matrilineal social structure that gave women a base of power (and protection from their uncles, brothers, and sons) from which to leverage provisioning help for their young from unrelated men, and to ensure that new alpha males did not emerge. (Knight stresses that, unlike mothers of other species, human mothers in prehistoric times would have had an acute need for provisioning help; he explains that, because the human child's large cranial size requires that it be born well before it is as self-sufficient as the newly born young of other species, its extreme and protracted helplessness would have been an enormous survival burden on the virtually "technology-less" human mother.) He further asserts that, in this initial human social situation, menstruation acted as something of a panhuman source of law and order—one the entire species could easily follow by universally scheduling the seclusion period at the new moon, and the conjugal period at the full moon. He points out that previous theories of human cultural origins have never adequately explained how humans overcame the constant fighting over food and sex that characterizes the animal condition; he further explains that symbolic meaning could only be sustained from one generation to the next in the absence of such constant fighting. In Knight's view, then, the lasting peace women's menstrual synchrony occasioned allowed for more complex cultural forms to take root and persist through the generations (122-53).

In proposing this model of cultural origins in which women initiated the exclusively human habit of sustained contractual exchange, Knight challenges the classical anthropological theory that men's trading of women was the first cultural act. Annette Weiner also sees women as culture-producing exchangers, focusing on the precious value of woman-produced cloth in many cultures—aboriginal, traditional, and modern. She notes that cultural identity is often derived from the cloth that women make due to its ability to "narrate" national, religious, or ethnic ideologies (Weiner 12-13). In her study of Oceanic cultures, she found that the sometimes supreme value of woman-made cloth comes from the spiritual power the people believe is inherent to women's menstrual and reproductive capacities (50-53). For example, in one Maori baby-naming ceremony—an initiation of sorts—the deity prayed to is a goddess of weaving and childbirth, who is classified as a swan maiden (an Aphrodite type) by folklorists (55). (Like the Aphrodite types, this goddess is associated with birds and with fine cloth/clothing; in her story, she is rescued from her abusive husband by her brother, escaping with him to a mystical otherworld, to which her husband later follows her, and where he stays and provides food to her family.)

With these initiatory traditions and anthropological ideas in mind, we can see in the ordeals, movements, and symbols of the Aphrodite types a common derivation from menstrual ritual and meaning. For instance, we can find a common menstrual significance in the Eastern dawn goddess' rosy and darkness-dispelling emergence from her bath. It also seems apparent in Inanna's civilization-initiating return from her harrowing trip into the watery deep on her Boat of Heaven (an epithet she uses elsewhere for her vulva, the marvels of which she praises as she leans against her apple tree before embarking to obtain the arts for humanity); and in the humiliated nakedness of her underworld descent that is both preceded and followed by her reemergence in fine raiment.

In *Descent to the Goddess*, Jungian analyst Sylvia Brinton Perera adduces the themes and images of the ancient sacred poem, *The Descent of Inanna*, to a Jungian psychology of women that conceives of women's bodily cycles and their attendant discomforts as periodic and potentially spiritually beneficial descents into and ascents out of a somato-psychological underworld. Using this insight, although not the Jungian approach, I view *The Descent of Inanna*, *The Courtship of Inanna and Dumuzi*, and *Inanna and the God of Wisdom*, as three stories of Inanna that most speak to an interpretation of descent myth as a code for women's culture-producing blood mysteries.

In her interpretation of *The Descent of Inanna*, Perera characterizes the underworld into which Inanna descends—the world ruled by Ereshkigal, the goddess of death—as

> . . . unbounded, irrational, primordial, and totally uncaring, even destructive of the individual. It contains an energy we know through the study of . . . the disintegration of elements, as well as through the processes of fermentation, cancer, decay, and lower brain activities that regulate peristalsis, menstruation, pregnancy, and other forms of bodily life to which we must submit (Perera 24).

She emphasizes that, while these processes involve physical trans-formation, the experience of them has a psychological dimension. In this view, Ereshkigal's death realm is an inlying reality for women that when, not ignored, can allow for a coming to terms with these implacable forces. Because of the myth's reverence for the death-in-life that all people carry, Inanna's self-risking descent presents us with the model for a dignified stance toward the inescapable catalyzing and degenerative processes of our bodies.

I believe that these poems, these earliest recorded religious forms, reflect what Chris Knight posits as the epistemological ground that menstruation provided in prehistory for the human understanding of the alternating natural cycles of life and death. Knight theorizes that the first apprehension of menstruation and ovulation as a repeating cycle was the material point of departure not only for a matrilineal social order, but also for mythological representations and ritual celebrations of twinned life-and-death goddesses. The religious associations of death with menstruation and of life with ovulation, made within hunter/gatherer cultures and recorded in the ethnographic record, as well as the same kinds of associations we inherit from our more immediate cultural predecessors provide a ground for such a claim. Moreover, the symbols, qualities, and mythic activities of ancient life/death goddesses can all be seen as signifying descent and reemergence from the menstrual initiatory seclusion rituals that are central to Knight's theory.

The identification of Inanna, the love goddess, with the fertile earth in the sacred poem, *The Courtship of Inanna and Dumuzi*—and her risky attainment of the building blocks of civilization called the *me*—in both *Inanna and the God of Wisdom* (the god also known as Enki) and, in *The Descent of Inanna*, perhaps point to a recognition by her worshippers that the abilities to plant, reap, and store crops in anticipation of winter, and the ability to plan life as an organized group were in some way connected to the evolution of the menstruating, ovulating, and sexually-active woman's body. (As in the ancient Greek myth of Persephone and Demeter, Inanna's absence from the upper world—the Earth—causes life and fertility to cease.) Indeed, Inanna's exultation in her vulva before she embarks for the watery abyss, the *abzu*, in *Inanna and Enki* bespeaks a connection between her cycles, her descent, and her reemergence with the *me* for the people of Uruk. When, in this poem the narrator says of Inanna's preparation to descend into the *abzu*,

> Inanna placed the shugurra, the crown of the steppe, on her head.
> She went to the Sheepfold, to the shepherd.
> She leaned back against the apple tree.
>
> When she leaned against the apple tree, her vulva was wondrous to Behold.
>
> Rejoicing at her wondrous vulva, the woman Inanna applauded herself (Wolkstein 12)

we can draw a parallel to her placement of the crown on her head before she makes her me-obtaining descent into the dark underworld, the *kur*, to meet the fearsome Ereshkigal (12, 53). For, while the focus of the narrative is on Inanna's death, resurrection, and her ultimate damnation of her ungrieving husband Dumuzi to take her place in the *kur*, her return to life with the *me* of the underworld is a crucial outcome of her risk. The sky god, Enlil, and the moon god, Nanna, both tell Inanna's attendant Ninshubur that they will not help rescue Inanna because "she who receives the *me* of the underworld does not return" (62). In both stories, Inanna miraculously defies what is either a law of nature or—in the figures of deadly sea monsters pursuing her in *Inanna and Enki*—what is tantamount to such a law.

That the wondrous beauty of her body (and her own appreciation of it) is so deliberately highlighted in both stories seems to suggest that her body is implicated in her success in both cases. Otherwise, the descriptions of the beautiful clothes and jewelry she is stripped of in *The Descent*, and of the youthful glee she takes in discovering her vulva in *Inanna and Enki*, both appear as a sort of nonsensical narrative effervescence. Given the narrative emphasis on her youthful beauty and her sexualized body, her impossible returns from below can be read as a storied representation of the "miraculous" bleeding-and-not-dying of the menstrual period. And, again, the civilizing benefits that her returns provide to the living might well be read as a mythic recognition of the ordering of life that Knight argues menstruation made possible.

Another parallel suggesting a connection between Inanna's body, her sexuality, and civilization is evident in that, in *The Courtship*, she calls her vulva "the Boat of Heaven," and in *Inanna and Enki* when she receives the *me*, she places them on the "Boat of Heaven" (37, 19). Moreover, at the end of *Inanna and Enki*, after she has docked the Boat of Heaven, we find that she has returned with extra *me* that Enki had not given her. The revelation of these *me* goes as follows:

> Then more *me* appeared—more *me* than Enki had given Inanna . . .
> And these, too, were presented to the people of Uruk:
>
>> Inanna brought the *me*:
>> She brought the placing of the garment on the ground.
>> She brought allure.
>> She brought the art of women.
>> She brought the perfect execution of the *me* . . . (26).

It is also important to note that one grouping of the *me* that Enki does give to Inanna is

> Truth!
> Descent into the underworld! Ascent from the underworld!
> The art of lovemaking! The kissing of the phallus! (15).

These *me* of love and sex, miraculously appearing upon her first consequential ascent, might suggest prehistoric women's readiness for marriage or conjugal sex that was offered (as Knight's theory goes) after the menstrual seclusion period (celebrated in the poem as her first consequential descent). In *The Courtship*, Inanna's cosmetic preparation for meeting Dumuzi—her bathing, perfuming, and application of amber to her lips and kohl to her eyes—are all (variously) fundamental parts of many, if not most, aboriginal menstrual rituals. Inanna's recitation of her cosmetic tasks and of Dumuzi's sexual attentions seem ritualistic, and appear to be carefully placed just before Inanna's decree of his "sweet fate" (44). This fate, in turn, is the fate of the people since he receives what appear to be kingly *me* from her. This also seems consonant with the aboriginal belief that the proper cosmetic ritual observances during menstruation ensure hunting luck and the happy continuance of the tribal cosmos. In *The Descent*, Inanna dresses, undresses, and dresses again as for marriage. The tripartite structure of this pattern implies a cycle, as does the pattern of the alternating descent/return at the end of the same poem, when Dumuzi's sister offers to take her brother's place in the *kur* half of each year. As mentioned above, when, in *Inanna and Enki*, Inanna is readying herself to go down into the *abzu*, she seems to notice the wonders of her vulva for the first time. This might imply that she is aware of her first menses or, mythically, that her first menses are the first, world-instantiating menses. Again, the *me* of sex and love that she gets from Enki and the ones she seems to generate herself, suggest that her world-ordering return from the other world is similar to that of the properly secluded menstruant.

Literary and artistic evidence from both archaic and classical antiquity, and ethnographic evidence in recent times, suggest that, while menstruating or giving birth, women in traditional societies have traditionally secluded themselves or were secluded. Thus, there is often a blurring of distinction between the seclusion periods and rituals surrounding menstruation and birth in myth. Perera interprets Ereshkigal's pains as birth pains, claiming that she gives a sort of rebirth to a newly *me*-empowered Inanna (Perera 37-42). This interpretation is consistent with the twinned nature of many of the ancient and prehistoric goddesses, the latter of which were often represented as two-headed or as a mother with a daughter on her lap.

The myth of Demeter and Persephone, the Greek variant of Inanna's descent story, includes images and themes from all three Sumerian poems: Persephone gets married; Persephone descends to an underworld with a river of blood running through it, and then returns with a pattern for civilized life; Persephone is trapped in the underworld while life on

Earth is threatened in her absence. One gloss of an epithet for Demeter is "Lady of Planned Society," a name that implies her responsibility (and Persephone's) for establishing human cultural activity.

In her book on the poems of the Sumerian princess-priestess Enheduanna, Betty De Shong Meador points to one poem's description of the purification ritual that follows the menstrual seclusion period of Inanna:

> On the seventh day when the crescent moon
> Reaches its fullness
> You bathe and sprinkle your face with holy water
> You cover your body with the long woolen
> Garments of Queenship . . .
> You fasten combat and battle to your side;
> You tie them into a girdle and let them rest (Meador 141).

Meador notes that

> Inanna's menstrual bleeding, . . . is synchronized with the dark phase of the moon. On the seventh day of the moon cycle, [her] menstrual period ended. Diane Wolkstein says of this poem, 'By joining the menstrual cycle to the moon's cycle in a monthly ritual, the wild, frightening, and disorderly parts of life are subsumed into a predictable and reassuring order.' At the end of the dark phase of the moon, Inanna's temper cool[s], and she lets her . . . rage subside and rest (Meador 141).

Saying more about the tracking of the menstrual periods of the goddesses in Sumer, Meador mentions the priests' actual charting at Ur of the menstrual cycles of Ningal, the moon goddess and mother of Inanna. She also cites Claus Wilcke's etymological work, through which he

> found the verb root for 'a menstruating woman' in the name of Ishara, the goddess Ishtar/Inanna in her mother aspect. Never a mother, Ishtar becomes Ishara when she gives birth in the great Akkadian creation epic, *Athrahasis*. Wilcke found the verb root *rs*, 'to menstruate,' 'to be in childbed,' switched in Ishara's name to *sr*. The related Akkadian verb *harastu* means 'to bind' and is used to refer to the cloth-binding used by menstruating women (56).

Meador also notes the signs of Inanna's eroding power and significance, as the emerging Bronze Age cultures increasingly marginalized women, increasingly organized families patrilineally, and increasingly glorified war and domination. She cites Enheduanna's voicing of Inanna's lamentations, as the male sky gods displace her from her temple and her city, and make of her something of an exile. It is in one of these poems that Inanna cries out for a place in which she is not an exile.

In my view, the universality—and the stubborn persistence—of the menstrual taboo only attests to the former status and significance of menstruation as a building block of human culture—indeed, as its foundation. Since that significance entailed a world organized to celebrate women's powers and safeguard their vulnerabilities, the current social order's dependence on the exploitation of those powers and vulnerabilities would, I think, be threatened by any change in perspective on what it means to menstruate. In writing *Lizzy and the Light Below*, I have made an effort to make what I learned in my doctoral studies accessible to everyone, especially girls who are about to menstruate for the first time, or who have just started menstruating. It is my deepest wish that it give them an abiding sense of pride in the significance of their female bodies, and that this pride translate to exquisite grace of action and purpose. I hope that by reading *Lizzy*, girls and women everywhere are better able to come out of exile, and to use their bodily powers to find the house, the home, the city in which they may fully live.

Jacqueline K. Thomas, Ph.D.

Works Cited

Buckley, Thomas and Alma Gottlieb. *Blood Magic: The Anthropology of Menstruation*. Eds. Thomas Buckley & Alma Gottlieb. Berkeley: University of California Press, 1988.

Friedrich, Paul. *The Meaning of Aphrodite*. Chicago: The University of Chicago Press, 1978.

Grahn, Judy. *Blood, Bread, and Roses: How Menstruation Created the World*. Boston: Beacon Press, 1993.

Guirand, Felix, Ed. *The New Larousse Encyclopedia of Mythology*. Trans. Richard Aldington and Delano Ames. London: The Hamlyn Publishing Group Ltd., 1968.

Knight, Chris. *Blood Relations: Menstruation and the Origins of Culture*. New Haven and London: Yale University Press, 1991.

Meador, Betty De Shong, *Inanna, Lady of Largest Heart: Poems of the Sumerian High Priestess Enheduanna*. Austin: University of Texas Press, 2000.

Perera, Sylvia Brinton. *Descent to the Goddess*. Toronto: Inner City Books, 1981.

Weiner, Annette, B. *Inalienable Possessions: The Paradox of Keeping-while-Giving*. Berkeley: University of California Press, 1992.

Wolkstein, Diane and Kramer, Samuel Noah. *Inanna, Queen of Heaven and Earth: Her Stories and Hymns from Sumer*. New York: Harper & Row, Publishers, 1983.

I.

Lizzy yawned and propped her chin up on her hand as she sat looking down at the curly-cue she was doodling. From where Ms. Duncan was standing at the back of the room, it would look as if she were watching the film. Health class was usually okay, but she had really been looking forward to this film, and it was turning out to be so strange and so different from what she had expected.

It was *the* film, the one about menstruation that everyone had been talking about since last week and that only the girls got to see. The boys had found out about it, and some of them had been saying gross things. But it had been kind of fun knowing that the girls could have a whole class that the boys weren't allowed to attend. Now, all of that seemed pointless, since the film was boring and, all of a sudden, menstruation didn't seem very special at all. It just seemed like one more thing to worry about.

"Is this all they have to tell us about it?" she thought as she glanced up at the cartoon girl playing tennis while she was on her period.

"Why does everyone make such a big deal about it and tell us it's such a special and important thing, and then all they do is show us a movie of how mostly our lives are just supposed to be ordinary when we have our periods?" she thought. "If it's so special, why are we supposed to pretend that it's not happening?"

Ms. Duncan walked up to the projector as the last of the credits flashed on the screen, and as she turned it off, she asked Lily and Lizzy's friend Sarah to start handing out the pink and white boxes that were on her desk. She had one for every girl. The bell rang just as Sarah handed Lizzy's box to her, and she opened it as they walked into the hall together. In it were boxes of different-sized pads, a package of powdered hot chocolate that had cramp medicine mixed into it, and some other products for menstruation.

"Is this all they give us?" Lizzy said, as she stuffed the box into the empty compartment of her backpack.

"Why? What were you expecting?" said Sarah, noticing that Lizzy seemed upset.

"I am so glad it's Friday! Hey, Liz, why don't you see if you can come over after basketball practice, and we can watch cartoons or something. Maybe you could spend the night."

Lizzy had been absorbed in some of her thoughts, but had heard enough of what Sarah had said to respond.

"Oh, I can't, . . . I have dance class in the morning, and tomorrow is my mom's birthday. Grandma's coming over later to pick up me and Chelsea so that we can make the cake at her house tonight. It's a surprise for Mom."

"She'll like that."

"You can come over, if you want. We're going to have the cake and a little party at around three, after my mom's aerobics class. Maybe we could go to a movie after that."

"Okay, I'll ask Mom. Oh, there's the bell—I can't be late for English again, and I've got to throw all of this period stuff in my locker. See you."

"Yeah, maybe tomorrow."

* * *

Walking into her world history class, Lizzy was still thinking about the movie and the box. She wondered why she felt so disappointed. It wasn't really the stuff she had learned about periods. That was kind of boring, but it wasn't bad or anything. It was more that there was something that no one was talking about, and it was the not talking about it that was so strange.

She was also feeling a funny feeling in her stomach—kind of an ache, but it wasn't as if she was going to vomit. She just felt kind of achy and tired. It all made her feel not quite like her normal self. It was a good thing that this next class was the last class of the day. It would be nice to go home and listen to some music or watch t.v. for a little while before Grandma came over.

She was opening her history book to get her homework out as Mr. Flanagan started class with his usual topic question:

"Have any of you ever heard the expression, 'History repeats itself?'" he asked.

Lizzy thought about it for a few seconds and slowly raised her hand, along with about half of the class.

"What do you think that means? . . . Can anyone think of an example of history repeating itself?"

All hands went down as everyone thought about his second question. She liked Mr. Flanagan's question. They always made her think of her own ideas. It wasn't as if there were only one answer. The first thing she thought of was war— it seemed like almost all of history was just one war after another, always over what seemed like nearly identical issues. But that seemed too obvious. So, she waited to see if anyone else was going to say anything. Amy Jackson's hand was the first to go back up.

"I notice that fashion repeats itself," she said. Like in the '90s, people wore vintage looks from the '70s. And now people are wearing versions of '80s and '90s styles."

"That's a good example," Mr. Flanagan said. "Any other examples that anyone else can think of?"

"It seems like wars keep happening, and one is always connected to the one before it," Lizzy finally said.

"Excellent point, Elizabeth! That is what we saw with World War I and World War II. That's a very good example. Now, let's talk about your reading assignment . . . ."

Even though she usually liked the discussion in Mr. Flanagan's class, Lizzy couldn't help tuning him out, first, because she was so proud of her answer and, second, because her stomach was still kind of hurting. It wasn't terrible, but it didn't hurt in a normal kind of way. In fact, the achy feeling was sort of blocking out some the good feeling she had about her answer. She forced herself to sit up straight in her chair and started listening to the lesson again.

It was an interesting discussion, and history was one of her favorite classes, but today she just couldn't give it her full attention. Several times, she was sure that Mr. Flanagan was just about to ask his food-for-thought question, and she started to close her notebook, but he kept on teaching. Finally, she decided to knock her pencil off of her desk so that it would fall behind her seat, and she could look back at the clock while she reached down to get it. This way, she could she could check on the time without hurting his feelings. Twenty minutes left! Time was going so slowly today.

"If history repeats itself, does time really move in a straight line, the way it appears to on the timelines we see in our book? Or does it really move more in a circle?"

He paused and then seemed to ask the air, "Does time have a shape at all?"

That was the question, and Lizzy nearly missed it.

* * *

She had been remembering a dream she had had the night before. In it, she was on a glistening white beach late at night. The moon so big and full that it seemed closer to the Earth than usual. So many stars glittered behind it in the deep night sky, she could see how they formed the swirl of the Milky Way. It was weird because, even though the moon didn't have a face in the dream, she felt as if it had been smiling at her and trying to tell her something. When she would look directly at it, she only saw its craters and valleys—but she felt that it somehow knew her and wanted her to be happy.

What was even weirder was that the moon was blood red. She also remembered that it seemed proud of her. In the dream, she kept walking along the beach trying to figure out why the moon cared about her and what it wanted her to know. As she walked along the sparkling shore, she noticed little starfish, sand dollars, and seashells half-buried in the sand. Then, near the end of the dream, she found a big spiral-shaped shell that was cut in half so that you could see how its regularly spaced segments had been the delicate pearly chambers of the growing life inside.

It felt as if the moon knew her and was trying to tell her something.

She usually forgot most of her dreams, but this one had been so beautiful and mysterious, she couldn't get it out of her mind. Her mom had read a book on dreams that said that it was good to write down the details of your dreams, and she was thinking that she should write this one down in her diary when she got home. Anyway, as she was walking out of class, she checked with Amy to make sure she had heard Mr. Flanagan's question clearly.

"The shape of time? That's definitely one of his most interesting questions yet," she said to herself as she walked back to her locker.

Once she got everything she needed from her locker, she was thinking more about the question as she stopped by the bathroom: "How could something that is not a thing have a shape? It's such a strange question. It seems like a question they would ask in college. I like how Mr. Flanagan thinks we can answer questions like that. I also like how he calls me Elizabeth. It sounds so grown up."

"Oh, my gosh, it's here!" she said when she looked down and saw the bright circle of red. "I've been having cramps. I can't believe that I would start on the same day that we saw that movie. I am so glad I put that box of stuff in my backpack after health class. Good, it didn't go all the way through. I still have to go home and change, though. I'll get the nurse to excuse me from practice and go home and call Mom. I can't wait to tell Sarah. She's not going to believe this. I want to get home fast. I'll cut through the woods by Dempsey Park."

II.

It felt good to be in the woods again. They were always shady and cool, and so quiet. She used to play here almost every afternoon with Angie Evans when they were in the fourth grade, before Angie moved. They used to pretend that they were prehistoric people who lived in the forest. It made her a little bit sad to realize that, after Angie moved away, she had stopped coming here.

Even though she still wanted to get home, the woods made her feel as if there weren't any reason to hurry. So, she decided to walk over to the fallen oak tree where she and Angie used to play the most. It lay just at the edge of an open meadow that was in the middle of the woods. (It had fallen over long before she and Angie started playing there—she knew this because, when Angie's older brother Danny and his friends were in elementary school, they used to pretend it was their army headquarters, and they were all in high school now.)

As she got closer to the sunny clearing of the meadow beyond the sleeping tree, she took off her shoes and skidded her feet through the thick grass so that the cool, delicate blades tickled between her toes. Dropping her backpack and shoes on the ground, and leaning against the old dead tree trunk, Lizzy closed her eyes to feel a soft breeze on the back of her neck. Drawing in a deep breath, she wondered if Angie still liked living in New York, and she felt bad that she had lost touch with her.

The grass felt so soft beneath her feet that she couldn't resist sitting down. Before long, she found herself stretched out on her back with her feet crossed and her head resting on her palms behind her head. "It's okay if I stay here for a little while," she thought, "I'm not really in a hurry, since Mom won't be home for a while anyway."

Lying beside the old tree on the soft grass, watching the clouds change was exactly what she had needed to do all day.

A reindeer turned into a dragon as the wind slowly pushed a puffy, white cloud across the sky. As she rested in the grass, watching the clouds change shape, Lizzy realized that she was feeling better. In health class, she hadn't understood why the film's narrator had said it was good to lie down sometimes when you get cramps with your period. But, she understood now. Lying beside the old tree in the cool grass and doing nothing was exactly what she needed today.

She wondered if female animals had cramps when they went into heat. She remembered learning in her biology class last year that most female mammals went into heat at least once a year, and that they had a sort of period then.

Lizzy really loved animals and wanted to become a veterinarian—maybe even for wild animals. She had heard her mom talking with Sarah's mom once about how sometimes girls stop doing well in math and science once they get into junior high and high school. She had made a pledge to herself then that she would never let that happen, no matter what. Becoming a veterinarian depended on it.

"I like math and I'm good at it. It's just a subject. It seems that people, even teachers, get an idea about it being so hard, and then can't see what it actually is. Then they just give up on it or give up on trying to explain it better."

Suddenly, Lizzy jumped to her feet.

"What was that?" she said to herself.

She had seen something moving, but it had run by so quickly that she couldn't tell what it was. It looked like a white furry animal but it was so tiny, she was sure that it was too small to be a rabbit or a cat. Maybe somebody had lost a pet guinea pig. It seemed to disappear into nowhere as quickly as it had come from nowhere. She saw it run into the rocky face of one of the small cliffs on the other side of the meadow, but she did not see it climb up to the top of the cliff.

"Where did it go?" she wondered, as she picked up her backpack and shoes, and walked toward the rocks.

"And what is it?"

She knew these rocks. She and Angie used to race up them. (Whoever lost would have to sing the yodeling song from *The Sound of Music* really loud at the top—neither one of them could ever get all the way through it, because it made them both laugh so hard.)

"It still has to be here somewhere, unless it went into an opening in the side of the cliff," she thought.

"But there isn't one . . ."

After looking for the little white animal or for its hiding place for a few minutes, Lizzy gave up and decided to turn around and head for home. Leaning against one of the rocks on the side of the cliff for balance, she pulled her shoes back on. As she pushed away from it to stand up, it slid apart from another rock, and she found herself looking into a small cave.

* * *

It was more of a tunnel than a cave. But, it was big enough for her to walk through if she stooped down and if she let her hands touch the ground when she lost her balance or when it narrowed. The air was cooler in here than it was outside, and she could smell moss—it smelled clean and was somehow energizing. Little by little, the tunnel got bigger, until Lizzy could stand up to walk, with space above her head. As she went in, deeper and deeper, the light from outside faded, and it was getting dark and a little bit scary.

As she continued, she soon couldn't even see her hands when she held them in front of her face. So, she started using her hands to avoid bumping into the walls as she continued. She knew she wasn't lost because, so far, she hadn't had to make any choices between different passageways. It was odd, though, because there had only been this one long tunnel that kept curving and going down. So, while she felt as if she were walking in circles, she knew that wasn't possible, because, if that were the case, it wouldn't keep getting darker. She could also tell that it kept getting bigger and going deeper.

She continued along the passage slowly and carefully and, after a little while, she noticed that there were pictures drawn on the walls of the cave. They were difficult to see, but she could tell that they were of people holding sticks, with large animals running around them. Before she tried to figure out any more of the drawings, she stopped and thought, "I can see these drawings because there is more light in here now. I wonder where it's coming from? Maybe I am close to another way out."

But the light didn't seem to be sunlight. As she walked on, she noticed that it got brighter and brighter, and that it was a silvery, sparkling kind of glow—it reminded her of the light of the full moon.

"I think the source of that light is just up ahead," Lizzy said softly to herself. Talking to herself out loud always helped her calm herself down when she was nervous or afraid. "Someone else must be in here. What if people secretly live in here? Maybe that little animal I saw is their pet."

Before she was able to get to close to its source, the light went out suddenly, and Lizzy froze as she heard footsteps coming towards her.

III.

"You are correct, my dear . . ." said the old woman, who had appeared suddenly when the light flickered back on, "I do live here, quite away from the world, and little Persephone is my pet."

Pausing, the lady looked around the cave and then looked back at the jar she was holding, and said, "Where is that Persephone? I am sorry she is so shy. She might come out of her hiding place before our time together is over. I do hope so. I believe you both would very much enjoy meeting one another before the end."

She was making tea, or what she said was tea, and she wasn't looking at Lizzy when she spoke.

"What does she mean by 'before the end'?" Lizzy wondered, feeling a little bit scared. "Maybe this lady plans to hurt me."

The woman had told her that she had rushed up to her right after the light went out because she was sure that Lizzy would be frightened and run away when the cave suddenly went dark. She had to put the light out to make sure that Lizzy was not an intruder—at least, that was the reason she gave.

It had only taken a second to get the light to flicker back to life, once she had assured Lizzy that it was best to come with her deeper into the cave. At first, Lizzy thought she was simply being friendly, so she decided it would be better to go with her. And, even though she got a little bit scared, now she wanted to know more about this very unusual person in this remarkable place.

They were now in what looked like the old woman's kitchen, sitting on small wooden stools around a little black pot that sat on a short metal stand over a soft and shimmering light. Even though the light lit the entire cave, it didn't feel hot and it didn't hurt her eyes to look into it. On the walls of the room, there were naturally formed rock shelves lined with jars and canisters of different shapes and sizes. In each of them were powders and mixtures of the stems, leaves, and twigs of plants that Lizzy did not recognize.

Turning to Lizzy with a cup of tea in her hand, the old woman smiled and, almost in a whisper, said, "Actually, Persephone is the one who thought you ought to come visit us. That is her job: to find the Changing Girls and invite them here. She loves it when one of you accepts her invitation. I am sure she will come out of her hiding place before you go, Lizzy."

Lizzy breathed a sigh of relief, thinking, "'before I go,' she said 'before I go.' Oh, good, that means that I am not being kidnapped or anything like that. This lady may be strange, but she seems pretty nice. Maybe if I stay I can figure out who she is, why she lives here, and how she knows my name. Also, I really want to know how she got that water to boil over that light."

As she took the cup the lady held out towards her, Lizzy asked "What is your name?"

"I am Luciela, Keeper of the Light Below . . . ." she answered.

Lizzy stared at her for a moment, trying to understand what that meant.

"But you can call me Ciela, my dear," she continued, as she picked up her own teacup from the metal stand.

Maybe it was the tea or the way the lady had called her "my dear," but just at that moment, Lizzy felt a wave of peaceful warmth wash over her. And just as the light in the cave seemed to gently mix with the darkness instead of making it go away, this warm feeling seemed to softly blanket Lizzy's other feelings so that she could understand them better. She didn't feel afraid of Ciela anymore because she wasn't really scary; she wasn't worried about hurrying home because Grandma wasn't coming over until seven o'clock; and the weird feelings she was having about menstruation (along with the cramps) weren't bothering her at all now because . . . . Well, she wasn't sure why.

It really doesn't matter why I feel better," Lizzy thought, "I just want to keep feeling this nice feeling right now."

They sat in silence for a few moments, sipping the sweet and spicy tea, when Lizzy looked up from her teacup and said,

"Ciela, what is a Changing Girl?"

16

The old woman's smile wasn't confusing at all now. Lizzy could tell that she was kind and that she even seemed to want to make her happy somehow.

"That is just the right question, Lizzy. I am so glad you asked," she said.

She paused, and, turning her face toward the light, she seemed to be looking very far away for her answer. Lizzy could see that she was very old and that her soft eyes were darkly shaded, even in the bright light, with deep lines them that continued down her cheeks. But, even though she had wrinkles and gray hair, she still seemed beautiful.

* * *

The old woman seemed to be looking very far away for her answer.

"Not only does a Changing Girl change from being a child to being a young woman when she begins to have her moon times, a Changing Girl changes her world. Month by month, year by year, your period is the time when you have the power to see the newness that life needs. And, believe me, my dear, it needs the new. What is the world without newness? It is the endless and dreary repetition of our patterns—war and suffering, a lot of unfairness, and everyone trying to figure out what's wrong and have some fun in spite of it all—year after year, decade after decade, century after century. It is history repeating itself—that is what it is.

Lizzy's mind flashed on Mr. Flanagan's question and thought, "How could my period have anything to do with history?"

Ciela smiled a faint, sweet smile and said, "Lizzy, I have some things to show you."

Then she stood up and walked around to the other side of the light. Watching her move across the cave, Lizzy noticed that she was taller and stood up straighter than most of the old ladies that she knew. Ciela knelt down quickly to pick up a lantern that was under one of the lowest rock shelves, and stood up with it just as quickly. She then turn to Lizzy, saying, "Here Lizzy, you hold the lantern window open so that I can light it."

She pulled a long twig out from a bundle of sticks and wood that lay next to where the lantern had stood. She held it in the big light, lifting it out every few seconds to see if it was lit. When it was, she carefully placed it inside the lantern opening until the light flickered brighter.

"There, now I will take the lantern, and we can begin. Come, Lizzy. Let us look at the pattern of life."

IV.

While sitting at Ciela's hearth, Lizzy had thought that she had reached the end of the cave. Because she could see a shadow beyond the wall with the shelves, she thought that there might be a little sleeping area behind it. She was right about the kitchen having an area behind the wall, but it wasn't little.

Once they had passed through a dark and narrow passageway behind the kitchen, Lizzy stopped suddenly and stared in amazement at the sight of the space beyond it. It was a cavern, really—bigger than any football stadium she had ever seen and grander than any of the cathedrals they had studied in history class. The ceiling was so high above them, and the floor was so far below them that they could barely see either one. It would have been scary were it not that a wide ledge along the walls wound up and down the entire height and depth of the cavern.

The walls were a glimmering golden-bronze color. And she could see that there were drawings and paintings on the walls all the along the ledge. This ledge also spiraled up and down as far as Lizzy could see.

The entire space was lit up by the same silvery light that had lit Ciela's kitchen, but Lizzy couldn't see its source. This light reflected off of the cave walls and created a sort of silvery golden cloud of light that illuminated their path as they began to walk along the ledge. Walking in this twinkling halo of light, Lizzy thought of stories about enchanted princess beginning mysterious journeys.

"Where does this path go?" she wondered, as she gazed up trying to see the top of the cavern.

As she and Ciela walked along the ledge—they were walking up—Lizzy began to look more closely at the drawings on the walls. She noticed that some of them were similar to the ones she had seen earlier on her way into Ciela's part of the cave.

"Who drew these pictures?" she asked, turning to Ciela.

"The Changing Girls and the Changing Women drew them." She paused and again seemed to be looking beyond where her eyes could see.

She continued, "But before there were any Changing Girls, I mean, before there were people, it was the Changing itself that drew the pictures."

"I don't understand what you mean," Lizzy began her question, "how can something that's not a person draw a picture?" Lizzy thought of Mr. Flanagan's idea about time having a shape. These ideas seemed alike somehow.

"I do not mean it actually drew pictures . . ." Her smile slowly fading, Ciela stopped walking and took a deep, quite breath. ". . . I mean that from the very beginning, the force of life has had a pattern that has appeared in many natural forms, and that this pattern has persisted as life has evolved, even up until there were people. The very first Changing Girls noticed that it was a part of their lives. The rest is literally history."

"What is this pattern?"

"Here, let me show you."

It was bigger than any football stadium she had ever seen and grander than any of the cathedrals they had studied in history class.

Ciela motioned toward the drawing on the wall next to where they were walking. As she raised her arm, the drawing changed from a very faint and ancient-looking etching of fish and sea creatures to a vivid, colorful, moving three-dimensional ocean floor scene. It looked like a hologram except that, instead of standing in the space in front of the wall, it seemed to be set into the wall as if it were a giant aquarium. The fish and sea animals and plants were enormous and strange.

"It's so beautiful," Lizzy gasped. "I've never seen fish like this before."

"That is because they don't exist anymore. These were some of the first of all the complex living creatures that evolved into the world of creatures that you know. Life gave birth to itself in the sea. There is even a clue about this in our words for the sea and things connected to the sea. The language family we belong to has very old root words that the modern languages use to form different words with related meanings. Our root word for the sea and things connected to the sea is 'mer' as in 'mermaid' or 'mar' as in 'marine biology.' It is directly connected to our root word for 'mother' which is 'ma.'"

"That's so cool," whispered Lizzy, as both she and Ciela stood silently gazing at the huge, neon-colored, sea-winged and crawly creatures making their slow-motion way through the jungle of sea plants that grew all around the colossal colonies of pink and orange coral.

"Look there!" called out Ciela suddenly. "Do you see that one there, crawling with its shell on its back? There is the pattern."

"What pattern, the same number of legs on each side of the body?"

"No, Lizzy, the spiral shape of the shell. That is the pattern. It is everywhere in life. It is the shape of the DNA in every living thing. It is the shape of light waves and sound waves. It is the form draining water takes, and it is the way high winds blow. It is the whorl of the galaxies. And, if you look at a spiral from the side, you can see the shape of ocean waves, which, everyone knows, are governed by the moon. So, would it surprise you if I told you that the spiral is the pattern of your menstrual cycle."

Lizzy looked puzzled. She could visualize every example Ciela had listed up until the last one.

"Does this have anything to do with the shape of time?" she asked hoping that it didn't sound like a dumb question.

"Oh, my yes, dear Lizzy. You know just the right questions, don't you?" She beamed at Lizzy and, again, Lizzy felt the warm feeling she felt before.

Ciela motioned with her hand again, but this time in a downward direction, and the fish and the animals stopped and seemed to turn to stone. Within seconds, the bright, teeming ocean world they been watching turned back into the simple prehistoric etching. Lizzy stood still for a moment, amazed by what she had seen.

They began walking again, and Ciela started to answer Lizzy's question.

"When women began menstruating, that was the very beginning of time." Ciela continued. "For, time only exists if it is counted. And, long ago, when women stopped having heat cycles like the other animals and began to menstruate, they also started to mark their moon times on bones and sticks. They were the first counters of time. They were the first counters of anything! Did you know that the roots of the word 'mathematics' are that little root 'ma,' which means 'mother' and the root for 'thesis,' which means 'wisdom'? Mother Wisdom—that is what mathematics is!"

"When did women count their cycles on bones and sticks?" Lizzy asked, curious about this connection between menstruation and math.

"Very long ago. Perhaps 30,000 or 35,000 years ago, in what is called the Ice Age. Early women . . ." Ciela stopped,

"Oh, why talk about it when we can see it with our own eyes?"

Lizzy hadn't noticed, but they had walked quite a distance from the "aquarium" drawing and were approaching one that looked a lot like the pictures she had seen on the way into the cave: these were of people holding sticks. As she and Ciela got closer, she could see that the people holding the sticks were women. They were sitting in the center of the picture in a circle. Other people were in the picture at different distances from them. Lizzy couldn't tell if the others were part of the same picture, or if they were in different pictures. They were just getting close enough for Lizzy to stop squinting to see the details when Ciela again motioned swiftly with her hand, and this picture instantly came alive. This one was much bigger than the one of the ocean creatures—so big that once it became three-dimensional, it looked as if it were another tunnel that they could enter.

And they did.

* * *

Most of the women were sitting around a little fire. It felt cold, and Lizzy wished she could borrow one of their fur dresses (she couldn't think of another word for the fur clothes they were wearing.) A few of the others, they looked like older women, were farther into the cave, painting new pictures. In the other direction, Lizzy could see the mouth of the cave and she saw some men who appeared to be skinning an animal. She could hear children playing just beyond them. The women who were sitting around the fire each had a little palm-sized rock in one hand and a little carving tool in the other.

"Do you see? They are counting their moon cycles," said Ciela.

"I can't hear them."

"Not out loud, Lizzy. They are counting by carving the days of their cycles into those little bones. Let's look more closely."

Lizzy hesitated.

"Don't worry, Lizzy, they cannot see or hear us. They exist simply as a memory of our beginnings as modern humans."

"But didn't people exist before the Ice Age?"

"Yes. Yes we did. But we did not really become different from the other animals until we began to have a complex consciousness. And that my dear, came with women's' understanding of the significance of menstruation."

"But, how could menstruation bring consciousness?"

"To understand that, Lizzy, you first have to try to imagine what life was like for these people."

They walked closer to the women sitting peacefully by the fire. One would murmur something every so often, but mostly they were quiet, intent on their work. Lizzy went near one of the women and looked very closely at the bone she was carving. She had expected the marks to be little lines marked close together like the ones in some of the cave drawings she had seen on her way in, but instead they were little moon shapes of different sizes—like the different sizes of the moon as it waxes and wanes.

"These markings are different from the ones I saw earlier. They're like little moons," Lizzy said.

"They are little moons and, if you look closely—it's a bit hard to see it at first—you will notice that the pattern they are drawing is a sort of flattened spiral shape."

"Maybe this was the first spiral any woman ever made!," thought Lizzy.

Lizzy looked again. Ciela was right, it wasn't obvious, but if you looked at it for a little while, you could see that it was a primitive-looking spiral. Maybe this was the first spiral any woman ever made! It was so exciting to see it up close.

Ciela continued,

"Before the unique evolutionary changes in the human female's body, human life was very similar to animal life. Women's bodies are the only bodies of all the creatures on earth that evolved to have two different organs that separate the reproductive function from the experience of sexual pleasure."

"This change, combined with standing up straight and the change from having periodic heat cycles to having monthly menstruation, meant that when women's bodies evolved, humans became free from the simpler, seasonal kind of mating relationships that the animals have. This meant that people were able to create deeper, more complex and lasting bonds with each other, gazing into each others' eyes when they were intimate. This possibility for enduring love was the beginning of human society."

"What does all that have to do with consciousness?" asked Lizzy, sort of understanding, but not completely.

"Well, when people got closer to each other and began to communicate and understand each other more, they started to notice and compare their experiences of the more complex patterns in their lives. One of these patterns was that women's monthly periods seemed to follow the moon's cycle from new to full to new again. Women who live and work closely with each other menstruate at the same time and, since people only lived in small bands back then, it made this pattern difficult for the women not to notice. So women started counting the days of their cycles and the moon's cycles. Did I mention that the words 'moon,' 'mental,' and 'menstrual' share the same root? It's 'me,' which means 'to measure.' This root is a variation of the root 'ma.'"

"When they noticed that when one cycle ends, it is only the beginning of the next one—like the seasons of the year and the growth cycles of plants—they began to understand that patterns in nature repeat themselves in different forms. Then they began to look for other patterns. What is most remarkable is that they began to see an even deeper meaning of these recurring cycles."

"... patterns in nature repeat themselves ..."
Ciela explained

"What deeper meaning?" Lizzy asked.

"They saw that this pattern of new to full to new again was a growth pattern—a survival pattern—not just for living things, but that it was a pattern of growth for the mind or spirit of individual people and of the community."

"Really?"

"Yes. They noticed that, as they tracked their own menstrual rhythms with the changes of the moon, their feelings changed at the different times of their cycle. They noticed that they often understood themselves and their lives differently at different times of the month. When they were ovulating— the part of the menstrual cycle that was associated with the full moon—they often felt more like visiting with people, helping and taking care of them more."

"When they were menstruating, they sometimes felt more private and thoughtful about their relationships, and about how life was being lived in their families and communities. They thought about what made them special—what they were good at—and about how they could express it effectively in the world without hurting others. They paid special attention to their dreams during their periods. This part of the cycle was associated with the new moon, the lunar phase that looks like the moon is hiding itself."

"How did this bring growth?"

"After spending quiet time during their periods thinking and dreaming about life, they would enter upon the ovulatory, more social part of the cycle with new insights into what was needed in certain relationships and group situations. With these insights, they could make the bonds of their families and communities stronger, and make life happier and more satisfying."

She stopped and took a slow breath, and looked at Lizzy to see if she seemed interested in knowing more. Lizzy's eyes were open wide, and she was leaning towards Ciela. Seeing this, Ciela decided to continue.

"The people in the community who did not menstruate— the children, the men, and the older women—considered this ability of menstruating girls and women to bring the new into the family and the society a very valuable gift. In fact, in some of the old cultures, the dreams of girls who were menstruating for the first time, the Changing Girls, were thought to be the most important of all dreams for understanding the destiny of the tribe."

"My dream!" Lizzy thought to herself, amazed. "This must be what the moon wanted me to know."

It was all starting to fit together and make sense. Lizzy felt connected to the moon and understood what it was trying to tell her in her dream. It was telling her that she was now an important part of the movement of the universe—the spiraling force of change and renewal. Her body marked the rhythm of life just as every woman's body has since the first woman started menstruating.

Lizzy was starting to feel proud of the fact that it was because of the changes in women's bodies that people started to understand life more deeply and build cultures. She especially liked knowing how her menstrual cycle made her have such a close connection to the seasons and cycles of nature. It was all so amazing.

"So is the part where we ovulate like summer and the part where we menstruate like winter, and the times in between like spring and fall?" Lizzy asked, ignoring her usual fear of sounding dumb.

"Another clever question. You are beginning to understand all of this, aren't you, Lizzy?"

"Yeah, I think I am. I can't wait to tell all of this to Sarah. She's going to flip! Ciela, I don't know how I can thank you for teaching me all of this. I feel so lucky that Persephone invited me. I hope I can come back and visit you sometime."

Ciela laughed a little and said, "But Lizzy, we have not yet reached the end."

"We haven't?" murmured Lizzy, a little embarrassed.

"Not at all, my dear." Ciela smiled sweetly and squeezed Lizzy's shoulder lightly.

"There is much more for you to see. Wouldn't you like to see more?"

Lizzy nodded and smiled back, even though she was feeling a little tired.

With each step they took out of the "living" prehistoric picture back towards the ledge of the cavern, the scene behind them slowly went still, its three dimensions changing gradually back into two. Back on the ledge, Lizzy could hardly believe that she had just walked inside this primitive, faded drawing.

Ciela brought her attention back to their conversation.

"Now, tell me, isn't mathematics one of your favorite subjects in school?

Lizzy nodded again, wondering how she knew this about her.

"Well, then, get ready to learn an ancient mathematical secret." Ciela smiled slyly and began walking a little faster.

Lizzy sped up to stay in step with her.

V.

After they had walked up another level of the spiraling ledge, Lizzy guessed that they were now walking along what was the math section of the cave, since they had already passed several detailed diagrams of how the marks on the lunar counting sticks followed the moon's cycle. She was starting to feel a bit more tired and little achy again, and her feet were starting to hurt a little. She looked down and couldn't believe how far they had walked; the opening to Ciela's part of the cave looked so small and far away.

From this distance she could see that the light had gotten brighter as they had climbed higher. They had traveled far enough up the ledge that they could now see much of the top of the domed cavern. Across the cavern on a part of the ledge quite near the top, Lizzy saw a rock bench that looked as though it had been carved out of the side of the cave wall.

"Maybe we can stop and rest when we get there," Lizzy thought to herself hopefully. "I like learning all of this stuff, but I would really like to sit down and rest for a few minutes."

As they passed more of the lunar cycle diagrams, she felt a little worried that maybe the mathematical secret Ciela was going to show her would be even more complex than these; and these looked kind of hard to understand. Her fear evaporated when she looked at the wall where Ciela was now pointing, and all she saw was a single triangle with a row of wedge-shaped markings next to it.

"Do you know what that is?" asked Ciela expectantly.

"It's a right triangle," Lizzy said with certainty. They had just started studying geometry in Ms. Alvarez' class, and Lizzy remembered this one.

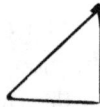

"It's a right triangle," Lizzy said with certainty.

"Yes it is," Ciela answered, looking impressed. "Do you know who is famous for his work with the right triangle?"

"Pythagorus," Lizzy responded easily. "He invented the Pythagorean theorem, $a^2+b^2=c^2$."

"That's right," Ciela said, pausing.

"Lizzy," again, she paused, "What do you think c^2 means?"

Lizzy did not understand this question. Again, it seemed like asking about whether time has a shape or saying that life draws pictures of itself.

"How could it mean anything, Ciela?" Lizzy said, feeling a little impatient and irritated. All of a sudden, she felt more tired and achy than ever, and really wanted to sit down. "It's just the answer to a formula," she snapped.

She felt bad that she had raised her voice a little, but she was starting to get kind of tired of everyone asking her so many strange questions.

Ciela didn't seem angry at her. She just looked at Lizzy for a moment and then responded,

"I know you take pride in being good at math, Lizzy, but really dear, you must understand that to grasp the feminine truths of math, you need to relax and not expect your understanding to be immediate."

Lizzy still felt upset, and Ciela stood looking at her, trying to understand what was still upsetting her.

"You do not have to be perfect, Lizzy," she finally said. "And you do not have to be perfectly nice all the time either. No girl does. Especially during her menstrual period."

"But, Ciela, you said before that it is up to the Changing Girls to make the world better. Doesn't that mean that we need to try to be perfect?"

"First, I did not say that you should try to make the world better. I did, however, say that the job of Changing Girls is to bring the new to light. There is a big difference between making the world new and trying to make it better. And secondly—and you must do your best to grasp this my dear girl—striving for perfection will only get in the way of your power as a Changing Girl."

"What is the difference between what is new and what is better?" Lizzy asked, interested in a distinction she had never heard anyone make before.

"There really is no such thing as "better" when it comes to the ways of the world. Approaching situations with the intention of making things better means that you are rejecting them as they are. It's a funny thing about reality—

it seems to respond best to our desires when it is accepted first and then worked with from there."

"When people have a problem, they usually decide that the circumstances around the problem are all wrong. Then they will often start doing things that appear to make the problem go away. But they have usually only made the outer circumstances go away. This makes them think that they have made the world better and, often, they have—but only temporarily. Usually, without knowing it, they have only set up a future problem with different circumstances. It is really the same problem; it only looks different. This is how one war leads to another. This is how we let the Earth be destroyed, bit by bit. This is how people keep suffering needlessly in the same ways, generation after generation."

Her voice had cracked a little as she said the last sentence, and she sighed and smiled after she finished speaking. But Lizzy could tell she was sad. Looking at the old woman's lowered, shadowy face, Lizzy felt her throat tighten. She wasn't sure if she should comfort her or tell her that just today in history class she had said something about how wars repeat themselves.

She decided to wait and be quiet as she reached over and touched one of Ciela's hands. Neither one of them spoke for a few moments.

Ciela sniffed and lifted her head, turned to Lizzy and began again.

"Now, ushering in the new, well, that is a different thing altogether. When I say 'new' I mean the insights that have never been seen before, the circumstances that have never existed before, the actions that have never been taken before. But they do not simply happen because we want them to—no, not at all—they come when we accept the discomfort and the limits of our problem situations."

"In the time we take to pause and reflect on just exactly how and why the people and circumstances that we do not like limit us, we can often understand more clearly what we truly desire. Somewhere between the truest sense of the forces that limit us and our hearts' truest desires is where the new jumps out to meet us and greet us, and take us into the changed world."

"It is not a better world, it is a different world where we are more deeply involved, more aware of our true place and our power to keep changing it from that place."

Lizzy thought for a few moments about all of what Ciela had said. It made a lot of sense, and she was glad that she had explained it, but something was bothering her. They had somehow gotten off the subject. Lizzy hoped it wouldn't hurt Ciela's feelings, but she felt that she had to ask her about it.

Quietly, almost in a whisper, Lizzy said, "Ciela, can I ask you something?"

"Certainly Lizzy."

"What does all of this have to do with math?"

Ciela look surprised and frowned a little. Lizzy felt that she had been rude and wished very much that she hadn't asked that question.

"Now, she is going to think that I don't care about what she said. I do care. It's just confusing because I thought we were going to talk about math, and I really like math and . . ."

Lizzy's thoughts were racing and she didn't know what she could say to make Ciela feel better.

"I thought you would never ask," Ciela said simply as she reached in her pocket, pulled out two pieces of chalk and handed one to Lizzy.

"Let's let Pythagorus tell us."

* * *

Taking Lizzy's free hand, Ciela led her up to the right triangle on the wall. Standing next to the drawing, she lifted her hand again, but the drawing didn't change. Instead, she drew a simple chalk line at the top of the triangle that was at a right angle to the hypotenuse (the "c" side). This line was the same length as the equal "a" and "b" sides of the triangle. So now it looked kind of like a Peter Pan hat with a feather sticking up out of it sideways.

She stood back and looked at the drawing and said, "Lizzy, draw the new hypotenuse."

Lizzy looked at it for a moment and then saw that, with the line she had drawn, Ciela had begun a new right triangle.

Only in this one, the "*a*" side was now what used to be the "*c*" side of the first triangle. Lizzy stepped forward and drew a new "*c*" side, a new hypotenuse.

Without a word, Ciela leaned over and drew another line the same length as the first one she had drawn, and again, it was at a right angle to the hypotenuse. And, again, it was at the top of the triangle.

"Your turn," she said to Lizzy.

Lizzy saw the new triangle that was ready to be made and added the line that it needed, the next new hypotenuse.

Ciela drew her same line again.

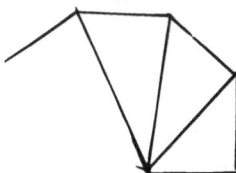

Lizzy drew hers once more, cocked her head slightly, looking at the connected sequence of regularly "growing" triangles they had drawn, quickly drew a few more, and then jumped back, her eyes wide with excitement, as she exclaimed,

"Ciela, there it is! It's the spiral!"

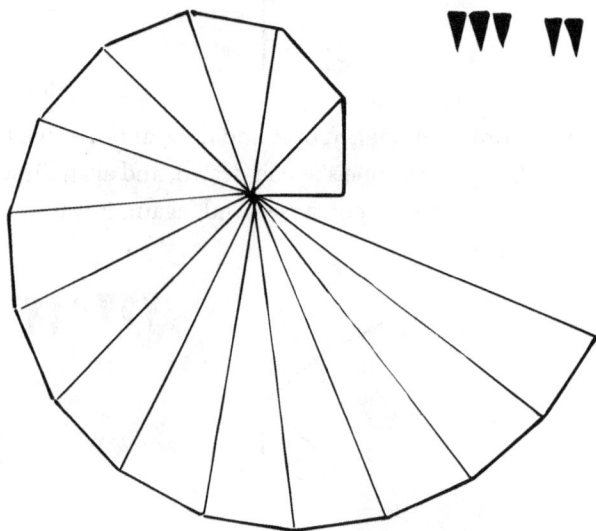

"There it is indeed," she said softly. And, after a pause, she asked, "Now, Lizzy . . . . What do think c^2 means?"

"It means 'change,'" Lizzy said plainly.

Ciela smiled and looked happy, "Yes, my dear. It means 'change.'"

"I wonder why none of my math teachers ever taught us this?"

"Because no one taught it to them," replied Ciela quickly.

"There is much of the early mathematics—the meanings and history of mathematics—that have been lost since ancient times." Ciela paused again, her eyes seeming to scan the space above her head.

Then, seeming to have found what she was looking for, she looked back down at Lizzy and began again.

"For instance, few people know that Pythagorus traveled to the Middle East to study math with the Babylonians, who lived in the area that is now called Iraq. Their number system, which they inherited from the civilization that preceded them, the Sumerians, is usually thought of as the earliest mathematical system on earth. Their numbers were called 'cuneiform,' which means cone-shaped."

"Is that what these little marks next to the triangle are?" Lizzy asked, looking more closely at the marks that she at first had thought were just decorations.

"Yes, those are cuneiform numbers." She paused while Lizzy looked at them and then asked, "Do they remind you of anything you have already seen?"

"Yeah, I was just about to say that they look kind of like the menstrual stick marks, just more regular looking. The ones in the middle look like the little crescent moons the women were carving. Did they have those counting sticks in the Middle East?"

"Some have been found there, yes. (Most were found in what is now Southern France—and it is said that Pythagorus also had teachers from that area.) Until recently, people who have studied the history of human development have believed that the mathematical system we have inherited simply sprang up over a very short period of time. Now, though, there is much more evidence, and it suggests that it was rooted in the older and long-standing counting practices of the early women who began by counting their periods and the moon cycles."

"I have heard that the Babylonians had a good understanding of math," Lizzy said. "Did they know about the right triangle?"

"Yes, they knew that there was some way that the hypotenuse came from a combination of the two sides, they just could not figure out the operation that made that combination. That is what Pythagorus discovered."

"Which operation?" Lizzy asked, so curious she sounded almost impatient.

"Well, . . ." Ciela gestured towards the drawing, "to get the length of the c side of the triangle, you cannot add, subtract, multiply, or divide the lengths of a and b. Before Pythagorus, people knew that c was some kind of combination of a and b, they just could not prove it with an equation using the four regular mathematical operations: addition, subtraction, multiplication, or division. Since a and b are the same length, they thought the length of c would be some fraction between the single ab length and the doubled ab length. What Pythagorus discovered was that there was a whole new set of numbers that could be used to figure out this problem. These numbers—the numbers that are created when numbers are squared and when the square roots of numbers are found—were what Pythagorus called the 'irrational' numbers."

"But doesn't irrational mean that they don't make sense?" Lizzy asked.

"That is how people use that word now," Ciela said as she put down her chalk on the ground, "but in Pythagorus' time 'ir-ratio-nal' meant simply that the numbers did not represent a simple ratio the way a fraction does. You know, the way that ½ means one part in relation to two parts of something. It represents the ratio 1:2."

"So, when you figure out the length of the hypotenuse, it comes out as something different than a ratio between the lengths of *a* and *b*," Lizzy said, pretty sure she understood. "It makes sense to me."

"Right. But it did not make sense to Pythagorus. Not at first anyway."

Lizzy wrinkled her eyebrows together and squinted her eyes a little, wondering what Ciela was about to explain.

"What most people don't know is that Pythagorus did not study math because it was a requirement in school or because it would make him better at business. He studied math because he loved numbers. Numbers explained the universe to him."

"Pythagorus and the students at the school he established saw different kinds of numbers as having different characteristics. When they discovered the irrational numbers, it shocked them and challenged a lot of their deepest beliefs about reality. They declared that what they discovered should be kept secret. Legend has it that when one of the students of the school revealed it to someone outside of the school, they had the student assassinated."

"How could a simple set of numbers get everyone so excited?" Lizzy asked, amazed that people could care so much about math. "What did they believe, and how was it challenged by the irrational numbers?"

"They believed that the world was ordered into opposites such as light and dark, masculine and feminine, good and evil, and so on. They thought that the even numbers were feminine and that the odd numbers were masculine. Since the irrational numbers (which were the square root lengths) were the result of the behavior of even numbers, Pythagorus described their spiraling motion as the "eternal feminine.""

"Was that what upset them?"

"It seems that what upset them was that this eternal feminine brought some inexplicable complexity to their simple, mathematically ordered world. They used to think that the number line, which in a way symbolized all of life to them, was a simple sequence of separate mathematical quantities. It was similar to how most people think of time now—as if it were just a simple straight line of one unconnected, identical, meaningless moment following another."

Lizzy thought again of Mr. Flanagan's question about the shape of time and then tuned back into what Ciela was saying.

"With the new lengths—the hypotenuse lengths—generated from the irrational numbers, they could fill in the little 'gaps' between fractions on the number line and all of a sudden, it seemed to mean that perhaps life was different than they imagined."

"Maybe it means that everything and everyone is connected— the way that life is interdependent in ecosystems."

"Why, yes Lizzy, maybe that is what it means." She was quiet for a few moments, and seemed to be thinking about what Lizzy had said. Then she began again,

"But they were not sure what it meant, and felt that they needed time to think it over and that it should be a secret until they understood it better. Anyway, once the word was out, the people who still believed that the number line was a set of unconnected numbers did not agree with the people who believed that the number line was all connected. And the debate has gone on through history, even until today. The people who do not like the connected view of the world have made the word 'irrational' into an insult.

"It seems to me that Pythagorus understood that the spiral shape was connected to women and to menstruation if he called the square root spiral the eternal feminine," Lizzy said, noticing that her sentence had turned into a question at the end.

"I think he did," Ciela agreed. "But, I should be clear that, because he saw the world in terms of such stark oppositions, he would probably have said that all women everywhere are essentially and only 'feminine,' which, to him, might have meant 'changeable' more than 'change-making.' Or, he might have defined femininity mainly in biological terms where women were concerned. That is, to produce a child is to introduce the new from two completely separate sources. I am only telling you about Pythagorus' eternally 'feminine' square-root spiral to emphasize my point that women have a special opportunity in menstruation to be very good at renewing the world. Not all women take it. Many simply ignore their menstruation, or worse, they feel ashamed of it.

Thinking about this, Lizzy added, "Maybe the ideas from the prehistoric people were still around in stories or songs—you know, the way that fairy tales and nursery rhymes kind of have old ideas in them. Could that also be a part of why he called it the 'eternal feminine'?

"Perhaps," Ciela replied, "but whatever the case was, I think it must have been exciting for Pythagorus to have found a mathematical representation of a pattern that exists in so many forms in nature. It is as if the spiral shape is a message or a clue from nature—it is as if it is the first, and maybe only, word that life ever spoke."

"And it is saying, 'Change!', 'Grow!'" Lizzy added, surprised at how sure she was of this.

Ciela smiled proudly and motioned to Lizzy that they needed to begin walking again. For the first time since she had sat in Ciela's kitchen, Lizzy wondered what time it was and if she was going to be late getting home. Usually, just the thought of being late made Lizzy anxious, but she sensed that Ciela wouldn't let that happen, and took a breath and walked on with her. She was still feeling tired, though.

Ciela began to speak as they walked,

"Many centuries later, a German philosopher who was familiar with Pythagorus' ideas reinterpreted this growth pattern when he said that history moves in a spiral. What he said was equivalent to saying that the two short sides of the triangle were like people or nations that are fighting. When the hypotenuse is found using the square roots of the sides, it is as if the deeper truth or essence of each side is drawn out to make the new length. With people who are arguing, finding the deeper truth of both sides of the argument allows them to get to a new moment in history so that the old moment—the old conflict—does not have to be repeated like a broken record." Ciela paused and looked at Lizzy to make sure she was understanding what she was saying.

"So if we don't find the deeper truth in a conflict, and history repeats itself, it's like we're going in circles instead of growing in spirals, right?" Lizzy asked, already knowing the answer.

Ciela nodded, glad that Lizzy understood.

"Have you ever noticed that sometimes you have the same argument over and over with someone?" Ciela asked.

"Yeah. Sometimes my sister and I fight about the same things," Lizzy said, thinking about the fight she had had last weekend with Chelsea. "Our fights always start out like they're about different things—like if she wears my clothes or my shoes, it makes me mad, or if she takes my CDs into her room—but we always end up yelling the same things at each other that don't have anything to do with the stuff we started arguing about."

"Well, the reason behind it is that neither one of you knows yet what truth your relationship needs for it to grow beyond this same argument. Sometimes it takes a while for that truth to become clear and it requires patience. The important thing is to remember that, usually, the conflict of opposites is in you first, and that whoever you are arguing with is, in a way, helping to draw your attention to it. It is also very important to remember that, as a woman experiencing the monthly opposites of menstruation and ovulation, you get special practice at understanding and resolving conflicting opposites."

Ciela watched Lizzy's expressionless face for a response. Lizzy was thinking about what Ciela had just said. They had been walking this whole time and were getting close to the top of the cavern and to what she had thought was a bench when she and Ciela had started walking. (It was a bench; they were close enough now that Lizzy could see it clearly.) As they had been walking and talking about time and history and math, Lizzy had been noticing that the drawings on the walls were getting fewer and farther between and, in the back of her mind, she was wondering why.

The light was now so bright that the shadows around Ciela's eyes were darker than ever—all Lizzy could see when she looked at them was a reflected sparkle surrounded by darkness. The lines in Ciela's face looked deeper in the light, yet her skin glowed more beautifully in the brighter light. Suddenly, Lizzy's random thoughts stopped as she stopped walking, turned to Ciela, and began to speak slowly and carefully.

"I think I am beginning to see what you are talking about. I think you are saying that not only does continuously going through the two opposites of ovulation and menstruation help us understand other kinds of opposites in life, you're also saying that menstruation makes us sensitive to what bothers us or what makes us happy. Then when we get close to our more active ovulation time, we can make the changes that our lives need, but in a way that doesn't make the old fights happen, and that helps us get closer to what we want."

She paused for a moment. "That's how we make the world new, isn't it?"

"Yes, Lizzy, that is how Changing Girls bring the new into life. They never forget that creativity is hidden in conflict."

"All of that from a simple mathematical equation. It is so awesome," Lizzy said, smiling.

"Why do you think they call it Mother Wisdom, my dear?"

VI.

"Lizzy, I want to talk about your dreams" Ciela said putting the lantern on the ground and settling herself on the bench. Sitting down had never felt so good. Lizzy leaned back against the cave wall, took a deep breath, and let her head fall slightly over towards her right shoulder.

"You do have dreams don't you?" Ciela asked, wondering if Lizzy had heard her.

Lizzy's attention came back from noticing how much more comfortable she felt to be sitting down finally, to her awareness that Ciela was asking her something about her dreams. Sitting down together, they were nearer to one another than they had been while they were walking, and Lizzy could now see Ciela's eyes again when she looked up to answer her question.

"I usually forget my dreams. But I did have one the night before last that was so cool . . ." Lizzy was ready to tell her how meaningful that dream seemed now, but Ciela stopped her.

"I do not mean the dreams you have in your sleep, my dear. I mean, What are your life's dreams? What do you dream of doing on Earth? What are you—the Lizzy who has never existed before and will never exist again—what are you here on Earth to do? Make no mistake, your nightly dreams are often very helpful in understanding your life's dreams. I would love to hear your dream about the moon. It is just that our time is growing short, and I want to talk about what you want to become."

A little surprised that Ciela was asking her this question (and that she knew that she had had a dream about the moon), but still not hesitating, Lizzy said, "I want to be a veterinarian."

"Oh, well, yes. You would make a fine veterinarian, Lizzy. You have a good mind and a strong, gentle heart. Yes, I can see you as a first-rate veterinarian."

This made Lizzy feel good and smile. She was about to tell Ciela that she wanted to be a dancer too, when suddenly—at the very moment she was about to speak—out of the bright light on the ledge above them, she saw a tiny, furry white face with big, round shining black eyes and a twitching black nose, shaped like an upside down triangle. Its huge pointy ears stuck way up in the air and seemed as if they would be much too heavy for its little head. Beneath its nose the round tip of its pink tongue was visible and it looked as if it were smiling from ear to ear. The light was so bright behind it, Lizzy couldn't really see the rest of its body, except she could tell that it had a very long tail. What was it? A dog? No dog has ears like that. But no rabbit has a mouth like that.

"Ciela, it's Persephone!" Lizzy almost shouted, but softened her voice as she started to speak, for fear of scaring the animal away.

"What kind of animal is she?" Lizzy asked.

"Yes, she has come to see you off. I think that saying you want to help animals was music to her ears."

"What kind of animal is she?" Lizzy asked, so curious about this odd little creature.

"Persephone is a descendant of one of the species that became extinct during the Ice Age. She is the only one of her kind left and, because she lives with me, she is able to live for a very long time."

"Can she live forever?" Lizzy stopped, realizing that in asking this question, she was asking if Ciela could live forever. This made her feel awkward and, again, she wished she would learn to think a little bit more before she said things.

Ciela smiled her sad, sweet smile again and said,

"As long as Changing Girls keep following her into the Below and as long as they do not run away from learning about the beauty and power of their changing bodies, she and I will live."

"Do some girls run away?" Lizzy asked, not believing anyone would not want to explore the cave, and stay and learn what Ciela had taught her.

"Some run away when the light goes out. Others just ignore Persephone or never even notice her." Ciela answered, her eyes glistening brighter than usual.

"But she is so unusual and so cute. How could anyone not notice her?" Lizzy asked in disbelief.

"That is a mystery we have not yet solved. She is a darling, isn't she."

"She looks so happy." Lizzy said, looking up and noticing that Persephone had moved closer to them—about halfway between where she had been and where they were sitting—and had curled up like a cat ready to nap.

"She enjoys a good story and she is getting ready for me to tell one. That is, if you would like to hear the story I have to tell."

It sounded perfect to be able to sit back and just listen. This would be the chance to rest Lizzy had been hoping for.

* * *

Ciela scooted down on the bench and motioned to Lizzy to put her feet up and to lie back. (Lizzy had slipped off her shoes and massaged her feet a little when they had reached the bench.) This part of the bench area had been carved so that it made a sort of lounge chair out of the bench when you put your feet up and lay back on it. Lizzy lounged back and became even more comfortable.

"Are you ready? Ciela asked, gently tickling the bottom of Lizzy's foot.

Lizzy wriggled her foot, smiled and nodded, closed her eyes and listened as Ciela began,

> *Inanna, a goddess in a Sumerian myth, was the first hero—male or female—in all of world literature. Recorded around 3,000 B.C., Inanna's myth was the first ever to be written down by anyone. Remember, the Sumerians were the ones to have the first number system that modern people could understand. In this myth, Inanna is the Queen of Heaven and Earth, the Goddess of the Living who*

must visit her sister goddess, Ereshkigal, the Queen of the Underworld, Goddess of the Dead.

As the story opens, Ereshkigal's husband has recently died, and Inanna understands that if someone does not pay respects to her during her time of mourning, Ereshkigal might demand more death than usual on Earth. Inanna goes down into the Great Below to prevent this, understanding that she is taking a risk: she knows that she might not be allowed to come back, since the law of the underworld is that all who enter must die, and that no one is allowed to return from the dead. Inanna enters the underworld, telling her assistant Ninshubur that, if she does not return in three days, she should go get help from the other gods. Inanna knows that, since she is the goddess of living things, if she does not return, all of life on earth will wither and die without her.

As she passes through the outside gate into the underworld, she asks that she be allowed to visit and then return to life above. Ereshkigal is enraged at this request and declares that, if Inanna has entered the underworld, she must obey its rules—dying as everybody else does and remaining dead forever. Since she has already entered the underworld and, therefore, has no other choice, Inanna submits to this law, hoping that Ninshubur and the other gods will help her get out. As she descends into the darkness, she finds out that, just as everyone else must do when they enter the lower realm, she must go through its seven gates. At each gate, she is told to remove a piece of her royal regalia, the signs of her power.

First she must take off her crown, which is a symbol of the moon and the stars shining meaningfully in the heavens above. (Remember, the moon helped bring mathematical meaning to Earth.) At the next gate, she must take off the lapis lazuli necklace that she wears around her throat and that symbolizes her wise and truthful speech. At the third gate, she removes the long double strand of beads that hangs down from her neck, signifying the way that all living creatures share the circle of life. At the fourth gate, she hands over her jeweled breastplate, which is a symbol of the beauty that we can make in the world by expressing our heart's true feelings and desires.

Next, she takes off her gold bracelet, which she wears to remind herself that it is important to make things with our hands, and to do the things that are important to us. At the sixth gate, she gives the gatekeeper her measuring stick, the symbol of her power to generate and sustain human civilization. (It must have had cuneiform numbers on it. Just think, the symbolic power of the measuring stick lasted from the Ice Age until 3,000 B.C.!) Finally, at the seventh gate, Inanna takes off her robes and humbly stands naked before Ereshkigal, who decrees that she must now die and be hung on a peg to rot.

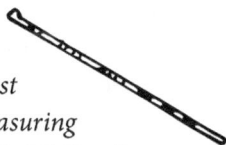

When, after three days, Inanna has not returned, Ninshubur goes to get help from the other gods. The first two she asks refuse to help. But the third god, Enki, the god of water, wisdom, and crafts, does agree to help. He immediately makes two little people-like creatures from the dirt that is under his fingernails. He gives them magical food and water to revive Inanna, and tells them to go to Ereshkigal and to show her sympathy for her loss. They sneak into the underworld and go before Ereshkigal, crying with her when she cries and moaning with her when she moans. She is touched by their sincere expression of sympathy for her sorrow, and she agrees that they can revive Inanna with the special food and water that Enki has sent with them. But, she says, she will only consent to Inanna's return to life, if someone else is sent back to take her place.

Once she is revived, Inanna goes back through the gates of the underworld. As she gets closer and closer the upper world, she stops at each gate, collecting her robe, her measuring rod, her bracelet, her breastplate, her long beads, her lapis necklace, and her crown. Returning to life on Earth, Inanna must decide who among the living she will send to the underworld to take her place. The first person she sees is Ninshubur, wearing dark clothes and weeping. When she sees Inanna alive, she is overjoyed. Inanna remembers that Ninshubur helped get her out of the underworld, and decides that she cannot send Ninshubur to her doom. On her way back to the palace, Inanna encounters her two sons, who are also dressed in mourning clothes and who have also missed her terribly. At the sight of their beloved mother alive again, they are thrilled beyond words. When she sees how happy they are to see her again, she knows that it also cannot be them who must spend eternity in the underworld.

When she finally gets to the palace, she finds her husband Dumuzi all dressed up in his finest clothes, sitting comfortably on the throne, enjoying himself without her, and reveling in his new and absolute power as the lone king. She is hurt and angered by this, and decides that he will be the one who should take her place in the Great Below. He tries to escape, but is caught by Ereshkigal's helpers, who *have accompanied Inanna to seize the person she chooses as her replacement. Dumuzi's sister Geshtinanna sees how afraid he is and, out of her love for him, offers to take his place below. Inanna asks Ereshkigal if this is possible, and she decides that Geshtinanna may share his sentence by going into the underworld half of the year while Dumuzi goes there the other half.*

Ciela stopped.

"And then what happened?" Lizzy asked after a few moments.

"Why, that is the end of the story, Lizzy," Ciela answered.

"What a strange ending. I mean, what happened to them all after the half-year arrangement was made?"

"Oh, there are other stories about these characters that the Sumerians wrote down, but this is the only one I want to tell you today."

"Why this one?" Lizzy asked?

"Like all myths, this one is like a code to be deciphered."

Lizzy sat up. This was getting interesting.

"A code?" she asked.

"Yes, the way the story is structured tells another story."

"How is it 'structured'?" And what is the other story?"

Ciela drew a quick breath and said, "Let me ask you." Then she paused.

"Lizzy," she continued, "considering everything we have talked about today, what do you notice about how parts of the story relate to other parts?

They were both quiet. Ciela looked down as Lizzy first looked up and then from side to side, as she mentally pictured the myth.

"It seems like . . ." she began slowly, "it seems like it's showing the two opposites of the upper world and the lower world, and how a lot of the characters have to go from one to the other at different times and in different ways."

"Precisely!" whispered Ciela excitedly, "And Inanna and Ereshkigal are symbols of those two worlds."

Lizzy smiled, glad she was getting it, and wondering where it was leading. She wondered this because Ciela had a look on her face that she now recognized—it was her look that said, "Here comes the really interesting part."

Lizzy was silent and waited for Ciela to begin again.

"Would it change the way you look at the story if I said that Inanna is also a symbol for the ovulation side of the cycle and that Ereshkigal represents the menstrual side? Does the story seem different when you think of these characters like that?"

Again, Lizzy pictured the characters. Then, after a few moments, her thoughtful look was broken by a smile.

"So, when Inanna goes into the underworld, is it like her having her period? And does her coming back and seeing everyone in a new way represent the 'new' that she brings back with her after her period?"

"Yes, Lizzy, that is one of the central meanings of the myth," Ciela said, glad Lizzy could think mythologically.

"There is more than one meaning?" Lizzy asked. Ciela nodded.

"Like what?" Lizzy wanted to know.

"Well, there is also meaning in what does not happen in the story. For instance, the fact that almost every main character except Ereshkigal makes a trip to another world is significant. Notice that even Ninshubur and Inanna's sons go from one extreme of feeling to the other—in a way they also go into the underworld of grief and return to the upperworld of happiness."

Lizzy hadn't thought about it, but it was true. It did seem like Ereshkigal was stuck in the underworld.

"Why is that so important?" she asked.

"Before this version of the myth was recorded, there were earlier tellings in which Ereshkigal was an upperworld goddess of grain and had another name, Ninlil. As a grain goddess, the only part of her divinity associated with the underworld was the symbol of the planted seed or grain."

"So when did the story change?" Lizzy asked, ". . . and why did it change?"

"No one knows for sure, but some people think that when a myth is recorded, it reflects the way the world is at that time. At the time when Inanna's story was recorded, the world was going through a strange transition. Many people will say that it is not true, but recent archeological evidence strongly suggests that in the older world—up until about 10,000 years ago—people did not build walls for protection from attack and there aren't any signs of mass violence or war. It even appears that people shared a lot more with each other."

"How much evidence and from where?" Lizzy asked.

"Much evidence. And from all over the pre-ancient world. But, Lizzy, we do not have time for me to tell you about these things today."

"But why do people say it's not true if there is a lot of evidence?" Lizzy asked, wanting Ciela to explain it all anyway.

"I think it has to do with the change that was happening in the world when this myth was recorded. You see, since this change, the world has not changed very much, and does not seem to want to change. One of the basic assumptions of the current system is that people have always used force and dominated one another. If there is evidence to suggest that this is not so, that things have changed from another gentler way of life, the current system doesn't really seem to want to hear about it."

"What was this change?" Lizzy asked, remembering that they were still talking about the myth.

"In just a few thousand years, a new way of being that was based on people dominating and enslaving other people was established. This new way of life was maintained with the threat or use of deadly force. The main idea was that life should be the way the forceful people wanted it to be. It was as if instead of accepting that life had these harmonious pairs of opposites like light and dark, summer and winter, ovulation and menstruation, the dominating people wanted only light and summer and abundance, and rejected that there was ever any value in experiencing the opposites."

"I can kind of understand why," said Lizzy, hoping it wouldn't upset Ciela.

"The people in the older cultures wanted abundance and ease as much as anyone. It is just that, to them, rejecting the opposites was the surest way to make abundance and ease go away in the long term. The more the limiting parts of life were respected and honored, the less limiting they would be. That was their philosophy."

"I still don't get why the myth changed. How did the grain goddess becoming the underworld goddess have anything to do with this new way of life?" Lizzy wanted to get back to talking about the story.

"Seeds of grain come from the dying plant and are planted in the winter. They lie still and hold the growth pattern or the destiny of the new plant within them. (It is not just a coincidence that in the underworld, Ereshkigal's assistant was named Fate.) If you have ever planted a seed, you know that, after you put it in the ground, you have to patiently wait and have faith that the plant will grow.

Patience and faith in the still, quiet part of the growth cycle were not a part of this new way of life. It was not respected. Only the immediately visible and quickly wealth-enhancing parts of reality were valued."

"So was Ereshkigal put into the underworld because she represented the still, quiet part of the life cycle?" asked Lizzy, starting to see what Ciela saw.

"Yes, Lizzy, she became a more remote deity, and was increasingly feared and loathed as a death goddess. But even after the new way of life had begun to be the law of the land, it seems that the people still understood that the dark side of life had to be recognized and honored. And that is why they developed this story. Inanna's descent to see her was understood as a big sacrifice."

"So if the new way rejected the dark side of life, then they must not have liked menstruation?"

"No, Lizzy, they did not. They began to associate it with evil, just as they began to associate Ereshkigal with evil, and the underworld with what is now called 'Hell.' They made up rules about how women were to be avoided when they were menstruating and stories about how menstruating women had dangerous powers that needed to be controlled. It was as if the old ideas about menstruation got turned upside down; instead of everyone respecting women's need for quiet time to contemplate life and their place in the life of the community during menstruation, women were now to be avoided. Instead of women returning to the active part of the cycle with the ability to renew relationships and do creative work, women now posed a danger to the predictable order of public life and were excluded from it."

"Why did they think it was dangerous?"

"Perhaps, they did not want anything to change. Maybe they felt that women's presentation of the new after their periods threatened the control they thought they had gotten over life. Perhaps they feared that the truth women told after menstrual reflection might disrupt their establishment of a world in which they could be comfortable all of the time. (In reality, they had only made other people more uncomfortable doing the work that made them more comfortable.) Why would they want anything to change?"

"It is strange how this change happened, and how much differently they felt about life than the earlier people did," Lizzy observed.

"It is strange and sad, really. Sad because many of the problems we have today—continuous wars, widespread poverty, and pollution—are rooted in this attitude that the limiting side of life is unacceptable. Strange because, when people go against a basic part of reality, they seem to end up embodying it—but in a negative way."

"I don't understand—how do they embody what they go against?"

"Well, even though the dominators pit themselves against the dark side of the cycle, they seem to continually bring a funny kind of change to the world—a strange and ugly version of the power that comes from the dark side of the cycle. Instead of bringing renewing change and healthy, although slower, growth, they seem only to bring a repeating cycle of ever more dangerous conflicts, an ever-faster pace of empty activity, with little time for anyone to stop and feel life.

"It is as if they planted a bad seed and it keeps on growing. And it is as if Inanna's fears have come true: remember, she worried that if Ereshkigal was not honored, more death and destruction would happen on Earth. The worst of it is that people—even the people who order life around the most—have a harder and harder time expressing their personal gifts to the world once they have felt life a little. I think deep down, everybody feels trapped by this way of life."

"Wow, it sounds so awful," Lizzy said, feeling a little gloomy, almost wishing Ciela wasn't telling her this part. This really was only more stuff to worry about

"It's not so awful when the Changing Girls of the world know what to do."

"But how can we make it any better." Lizzy stopped herself. She knew what Ciela was going to say.

"Oh, we must not try to make it better." She began, smiling because she knew Lizzy knew what she was going to say.

"Our power is in accepting the situation as a limitation and working from there to change it creatively. Starting always with our own lives, we can reintroduce the idea that nothing that we perceive as bad is unworkable or unchangeable. The seed of what we most desire often lies still and silent, hidden in situations that seem completely undesirable. Finding and nurturing this seed is how we bring real change and growth. Our sensitivity during our menstrual times is the key to our understanding of what needs to change and how we can change it. Our high energy and connection to others during our ovulation helps us make it real. Then, during the following menstrual time, we look back at what we have done and re-evaluate what we have accomplished, and decide what still needs to change or be changed differently. Doing this kind of change work will guide us to the way that we can best express our particular gifts to the world. This is what we do best!"

At that very moment, Persephone, who had come nearer and nearer as they had been talking, jumped up and landed gently in Lizzy's lap. Lizzy laughed, happy to finally get to see her close up.

"Hi there!" She said to the tiny creature, smiling and petting the soft fur behind her ears with her fingertips.

"Now, I'll never be able to leave." Lizzy whispered, giggling.

Circling around on Lizzy's lap a few times and finally finding just the right spot, Persephone curled herself up into a fluffy white ball and began another nap.

"Now, I'll never be able to leave." Lizzy whispered, giggling, to Ciela.

"Do not let her fool you. She is not just taking a nap. She knows it is just about time for you to go, and she is taking her place for the ceremony."

Lizzy gazed at Ciela wondering what she was talking about. Before she could form the words of her question about it, Ciela whispered,

"Lizzy, I would like you to close your eyes."

Lizzy closed her eyes, sat up a little and touched Persephone to let her know that she wasn't going to stand up.

Ciela continued, "Your moon time has come, Lizzy, and you have met the challenge of understanding its significance. You are now ready to return to the world as a Changing Girl. I have some things to give you and some words to say as a blessing so that you will never forget what every girl needs to know: your period is your connection to your destiny, and the first day of your first period is truly a sacred day."

Lizzy kept her eyes closed and heard Ciela moving away from the bench. This was so nice of Ciela, but Lizzy had never had anyone give her a ceremony before, and the thought of it was making her feel kind of nervous. Maybe she wouldn't do it right or know how to act.

VII.

Darkness. That's what she saw when she opened her eyes. The light in the cave had gone out again as suddenly as it had right before she had met Ciela. Ciela had walked away from the bench with the lantern and was now returning with it hanging from one hand, as she carried a rather large, interesting looking box in the other. A moving circle of light from the lantern enveloped her as she walked.

When she reached the bench, she placed the box next to Lizzy, stood directly in front of her, leaned over a little and delicately placed her two hands around Lizzy's upturned face. Smiling her gentle smile, she began to speak.

"Lizzy, you have a precious gift to offer to the world, and it is unlike the gift of any other. For there has never been, is not now, nor will there ever be another you. Finding and expressing the true, unfolding uniqueness of your gift will be easier when you use the renewing power that comes from honoring your menstrual period. You are . . ."

"Wait, Ciela. **Stop!**" Lizzy looked terrified, shocked that she had almost shouted.

"Lizzy, what is the matter?" Ciela asked, sitting down beside her and putting her arm around her shoulders, afraid that Lizzy was ill or in pain.

". . . you have a precious gift to offer to the world."

"Ciela, I'm so sorry. I don't want to be rude or hurt your feelings, but . . . it's just that, well, I really have enjoyed learning so much about menstruation and history, and everything that you have been teaching me, but, well, . . . I feel like I'm being kind of fake, and I just can't go through with this."

"Fake?" Ciela repeated her word, not understanding.

"Well, it's just that even though I understand that menstruation is really important and even inspirational, it is still kind of hard to think that it's so great. I mean, I have been feeling tired and achy, and just kind of bad all day. And, honestly, I don't like it. Also, you have to admit, dealing with a period is kind of gross. I'm sorry I didn't say anything about it before, but I was afraid to tell you that I have been feeling like this."

"Oh, is that what is bothering you? Well, I can certainly understand those feelings. They are completely natural feelings to have. A period can be very uncomfortable—even painful and messy—and sometimes so inconvenient. And we have covered a lot of ground in a short time today. You must be worn out. I am so sorry. I knew that you were in a hurry, and I was trying to rush through so much information. Oh, please forgive me, Lizzy. I have not truly been honoring your period."

Lizzy was surprised that Ciela was apologizing to her.

"So you don't think I am being fake even though I feel that way about it a little?"

"Not at all. I think you have proven that you truly are a Changing Girl—you felt your real feelings and expressed them honestly. You did not go through with the ceremony to please me. That took courage."

Ciela smiled and touched Lizzy's cheek just in time to catch a trailing tear on one of her fingertips.

"You are crying, Lizzy. Are you sad?"

"Oh, Ciela, it is so nice to be here. I feel so much like my real self with you. Being here, it seems like my hopes and dreams matter so much. I wish I didn't have to leave."

"But it is precisely because your hopes and dreams matter so much that you must leave. The world needs your gifts!"

She paused, and then asked, "Would you like to continue the ceremony?"

Lizzy took a deep breath, and smiled and nodded as she wiped away the other tears that had fallen down her cheeks. Ciela reached over and picked up the box that she had placed on the bench earlier and began to remove the lid. Suddenly, she stopped, put the box back on the bench, turned to Lizzy and said, "Before we begin, I would like to talk a little bit more about the unpleasantness of menstruation."

She stopped talking as she put the box back on the bench. (She had only put the lid back on halfway, and Lizzy sat up, turned her head a little and looked down to see if she could see what was inside.) She looked back at Ciela, who was looking at Lizzy to see if she should continue. Lizzy opened her eyes wider, signaling to Ciela that she wanted to listen again.

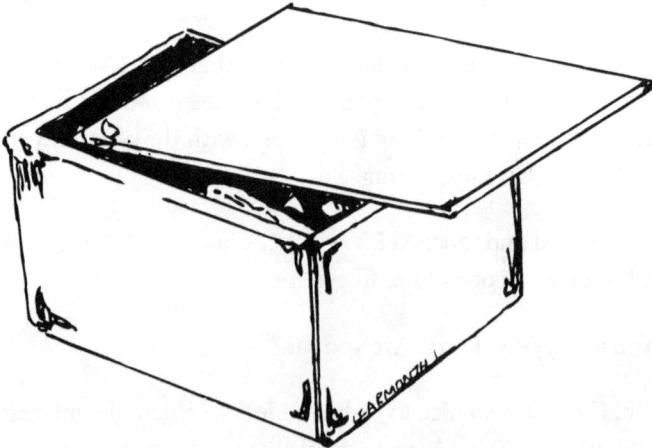

Ciela smiled and began,

"While some women barely notice their periods and no two periods are the same for any woman, the discomfort that most women feel at menstruation can be very valuable. For many of us, every month for much of our lives, our menstruation reminds us that there is suffering in life. When we have sympathy and compassion for ourselves—for our sensitive, menstruating bodies—we gain the ability to readily feel sympathy and compassion for others who are suffering. Do you remember how Inanna went into the underworld willingly for the good of all living beings?"

Lizzy nodded again, remembering that going into the underworld was a mythic code that meant that Inanna was having her period.

Ciela continued, "Some women notice that when their periods are the most uncomfortable, they are often unhappy about some of the circumstances of their lives. It is as if their periods are trying to tell them that something is wrong and that it is time, or maybe even past time, to change things. These are two very valuable functions of menstrual discomfort. Viewing the unpleasant side of menstruation as an experience that brings compassion and a deeper understanding of life makes it seem even more beautiful to me."

"I can see what you mean, but if it hurts really bad shouldn't we just take something to kill the pain?" Lizzy asked.

"Well, maybe, if it is terrible, terrible pain. But maybe killing the pain immediately before exploring its meaning means killing something else entirely." Ciela responded.

Lizzy looked puzzled. Ciela went on,

"I do not mean to say that we should not alleviate pain. That is the whole point of having compassion. Compassion motivates us to help alleviate our own pain and the pain we see around us. It is similar to what we were talking about earlier when we talked about the old and new ways of thinking—killing pain often seems tantamount to sending it into the underworld where it can be forgotten. If it is forgotten, it cannot bring any change to a suffering world. Just think, dealing maturely with the messiness and discomfort of your period might be very good training for helping sick and injured animals or for handling emergencies. And it is possible to get relief from menstrual discomfort through gentler means. There are exercises, nice herbal combinations, and other compounds that help immensely."

What Ciela was saying was making more sense than ever to Lizzy. All of a sudden, the way she had been feeling seemed kind of babyish to her. Even though she had understood everything Ciela had been teaching her about becoming a young woman, now, for the first time since she had been in Ciela's world—for the first time in her life, really—Lizzy knew that she was having grown-up feelings. The fact that her body had so much to do with made it seem magical to her.

Ciela had finished speaking and was looking at Lizzy, who wasn't smiling or frowning, but was looking off into the space behind Ciela. Ciela wondered if she had said too much and was worried that what she had said had been too serious for Lizzy. They were still and silent for a few moments.

"Ciela, . . ." Lizzy said, almost whispering.

"Yes, dear?"

"I am ready for the ceremony whenever you are."

"Oh, that is marvelous, Lizzy!" she exclaimed, barely able to contain her joy. She could tell that Lizzy really meant it this time.

VIII.

"All right, then . . ." Ciela began, "I would like you to close your eyes again. And please lie back again, if that would make you feel more comfortable."

Lizzy leaned back against the wall and closed her eyes, took another deep breath and listened for Ciela to begin.

"Now, my dear, I want you to imagine that, like Inanna, you are going down into the underworld for the first time, dressed in your royal robes and regalia. You enter through a secret opening in the Earth, not knowing the way and not knowing what you will find as you go.

"Just beyond the entrance, you find a steep and narrow stairway. You begin to walk slowly, step by step, down these stairs. As you continue down into this unknown world, it gets darker and darker the farther you go. There are several landings on this staircase. You stop at each one for a moment to remove your regalia, piece by piece.

"At the first landing, you take off your crown. As you place it on the ground, you notice that it keeps sparkling even in the almost total darkness. Slowly and carefully, you continue down the stairs. You come to the next stopping place, unclasp your necklace and place it on the ground. You are surprised to see it lie on the floor in a perfect circle, since you did not try to make it so.

"Walking on, going down the stairs one step at a time, you get to the next landing, where you put down your measuring stick. When you look at it lying there, the little moon markings on the stick seem to come alive and turn into numbers and letters that begin an intricate, joyous dance with one another. As they jump together and move apart, they form sets and equations—they are having fun making math. You remove the other parts of your finery at the next few landings.

"Once you have removed every piece, you stand there alone at the bottom of the stairs in the deepest part of the underworld aware of your body as the basis of your earthly existence. You let a tide of love and respect for your precious and powerful body wash over you. You know that these feeling of acceptance of your body are the source of the creative work you will do in the world. You know that cherishing your body and its monthly process will allow you to know your heart's desire and to follow it.

"You stop to consider that your uterus is very much like your heart: not only is it made up of the same kind of smooth muscle as the heart, it fills up with blood and then pushes the blood out, over and over again in a natural and regular rhythm, just as the heart does. And, just as the rhythm of your sensitive, beating heart helps you find your way, the rhythm of your uterus—the rhythm of your menstrual cycle—helps you feel your way through life. You know that your best work will come from being true to these deep, natural feelings. You know that no one else can do your work because there is no one else like you, and there never will be. Most importantly, you know that the world needs your gifts."

Ciela paused, listened to Lizzy's breathing to make sure that she hadn't fallen asleep, and then began again,

"You stand there a little while longer, not knowing what will happen and then, out of the dark silence, you hear a soft, deep voice beckoning you to come close. You look out into the blackness and see a little distance away only the sparkling of two kind eyes. You cannot really understand the words this voice is saying, but you understand its meaning. It is telling you that it has a gift for you. You walk towards the two eyes and as you approach, they disappear into the darkness. As you get to the place where they once were, you look down and on the ground, in the dim light, you see the gift that has been left for you."

Ciela paused and looked down at Lizzy. Lizzy's face looked so perfectly relaxed, Ciela thought that she had never seen such a sweet face.

"Lizzy?" Ciela whispered. Without opening her eyes, Lizzy answered softly, "Yes?"

"Let your imagination show you your gift from the underworld."

They were silent for a few moments.

"Do you see it?" Ciela asked, hoping not to rush her.

"Yes, I can see it" Lizzy murmured.

"Wonderful," Ciela said, still whispering, "Now, imagine picking up your gift and, when you are ready, turning around and beginning your journey back to the world above. As you leave the underworld, the light begins to get brighter with each step you take up the stairs. As you go higher and higher, you stop at each landing and take back each piece of your regalia, understanding the meaning of each piece more deeply than ever."

"When you get to the top of the stairs and begin walking towards the opening to the upperworld, you are wearing your necklace and crown and the rest of your regalia. You are holding your measuring stick and the gift you have been given. You have made your first journey to the underworld and back, you see that the sun is shining as you reach the doorway. You walk through the door knowing that the world needs you.

Again Ciela paused and looked at Lizzy's peaceful face. "You can open your eyes when you are ready, Lizzy."

Lizzy slowly blinked and opened her eyes the slightest bit at first. The light in the cavern was getting brighter by the second, and Lizzy noticed that it was now mixed with the lantern light. When her eyes had adjusted to the light, she opened them up completely, still blinking.

"What was your gift?" Ciela asked, excited to know what underworld treasure Lizzy had received.

"What?" Lizzy asked, still not completely back from her imaginary journey.

"The gift from your imagination," Ciela replied quickly. "What was on the floor of your underworld?"

"Oh, it was actually two things. One was a stethoscope and one was a pair of dance shoes. Isn't that a funny combination?"

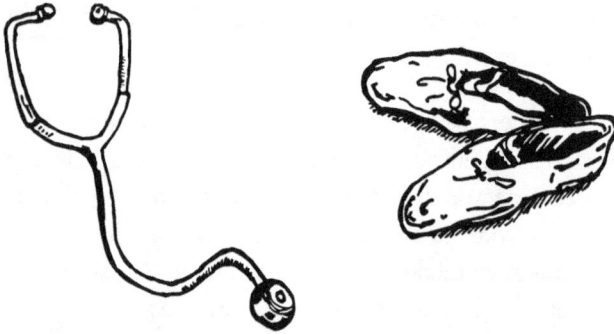

"But it is perfect for a girl who wants to be a veterinarian and a dancer!" Ciela exclaimed.

Lizzy smiled and wondered again how Ciela could know so much about her, especially the things that were most important to her. She had never mentioned that she wanted to be a dancer.

"Ciela, how do you know all these things about me, like my name and what I want to be, and that I like math?" Lizzy had to ask.

"I know these things in the same way that your imagination knows what gifts to give you, and in the same way your body knows when it is time to change. I know you and about you because your mind is now connected to the moon mind of all women."

The way Ciela said this sounded so lovely, and it reminded her of the way the moon seemed to know her in her dream.

She sat there silently for a few moments, remembering the image of its warm red glow.

Lizzy refocused her eyes as she noticed that Ciela was reaching over beside her to pick up the box she had brought before beginning the ceremony. Wanting to help Ciela by handing it to her, Lizzy also reached over to pick it up. She picked it up before she got a good grip on it and accidentally tipped it over, spilling everything in it out onto the bench. Lizzy gasped, terrified that she had broken something.

"Oh, Ciela, I am so sorry! I can't believe I did that."

"Heavens, dear Lizzy, there is no harm done. Things spill sometimes and, besides, these are gifts for you, and none of them is broken."

Relieved, Lizzy sighed and, then replaying in her mind what Ciela had just said, she looked down the scattered little pile of sparkling, mysterious objects.

As Lizzy gazed at her gifts, Ciela reached down and picked up what at first looked like a rock. As she handed it to her, Lizzy could see that it was a fossilized spiral-shaped shell.

"Ciela, a fossil! It's so cool! How old is it?"

"Many millions of years old," Ciela answered, happy that Lizzy recognized what it was.

"This isn't as old, but it is just as precious," Ciela said as she took out another little rock-sized object.

"It's one of the counting bones! Oh, wow! I get to keep this?"

Ciela nodded.

"Thank you so much. I feel so lucky!"

"You are quite welcome, my dear. But there is no better person than you to have it. One thing I did not tell you about these bones and sticks is that they are the predecessors of the scepters of royalty. (The word we have for a measuring stick—a ruler—attests to this connection.) So, as you hold it, let it remind you of the original power it represents."

Ciela reached down again and picked up a necklace with a moon-shaped pendant, and held it out to Lizzy, motioning her to turn her head around so that she could clasp it around her neck.

"This moon hanging at your throat can serve as a reminder to speak your truth and to speak up for what you want. Let your voice be heard, dear Lizzy, and know that, sometimes, it is very powerful to say nothing at all."

Lizzy was looking down at the pretty necklace and was just about to thank Ciela again, when she looked up and gasped. Ciela held out a beautiful sparkling tiara, ready to put it on Lizzy's head.

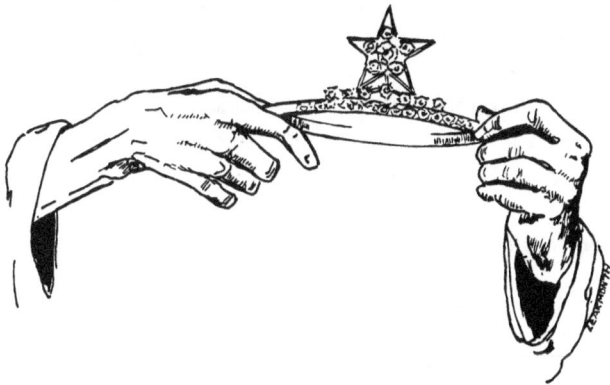

"Lizzy, I am placing this crown on your head as a symbol of the moon shining above you. I want you to remember that the moon's meaning, the moon's rhythm is a source of power for you and for all Changing Girls and Changing Women."

Lizzy didn't know what to say. She had always thought crowns and tiaras were kind of dumb. Beauty pageants had always seemed so strange, and the girls who entered them so empty and silly. But thinking of a tiara the way that Ciela was describing it made it sound so wonderful. Like this was the original meaning of crowns, and that somewhere along the way in history, it had become meaningless because everyone had forgotten about this part of women's importance in the world.

"Ciela, I love it. I don't know how to thank you. I can't wait to show Mom and Grandma, and Chelsea and my friend, Sarah."

"Again, my dear, you are most welcome. I am so glad you like these things. You can tell Sarah and Chelsea that they are welcome to come for their gifts when their changing times come. Tell them to follow any funny little white animals they see running past them!"

They both laughed a little and then looked down and became quiet for a few moments. The light had gotten very bright again. Lizzy sighed and looked up, asking,

"Ciela it's time for me to go now, isn't it?"

"Yes. Yes it is." Ciela said, a smile returning to her lips.

"But before you go, I have one more thing for you. Actually, I have one for you and one for your mother."

"Really? What is it?"

Ciela reached into the box once more and took from it what looked like two stalks of wheat.

"Is that wheat?" Lizzy asked, reaching up and carefully taking hold of the two delicate stalks.

"It is wheat." Ciela answered simply, pretty certain that Lizzy would understand its significance.

"I know what it's for. It represents my dreams and the way that they can become reality if I pay attention to them. Like how if you plant a seed, you have to water it and take care of the plant as it grows."

"That's right, Lizzy. It is a symbol of your destiny. When you give your mother her wheat stalk, let her know that it can serve to remind her of the dreams she has always had."

"I can give it to her tomorrow for her birthday!"

Thinking of it as a birthday present made it seem even better.

"Here, Lizzy, let's put your things back into your box. Persephone and I must go back now."

She and Ciela began carefully placing the symbolic objects back into the box one by one. Lizzy held on to the wheat.

The thought of Ciela leaving her made her sad. She knew she had to get home and wished Ciela could come with her. Why did she have to stay down here?

"Ciela, how do I get out of here?" Ciela was silent.

"Can't you show me the way out and come with me? . . . Do you have to stay here? . . . Can I come back and visit sometime?"

Lizzy thought that if she kept asking questions, Ciela would start walking and talking with her again.

The light was getting still brighter, and Ciela's eyes were again becoming hard to see in their shadows. She was slowly moving away from Lizzy with the saddest smile Lizzy had ever seen. Suddenly, Persephone sat up in her lap, looking at Lizzy with her huge black eyes.

Lizzy looked down at her and softly stroked her little head.

"Thank you for inviting me, Persephone. You did a good job of getting my attention," Lizzy said, trying to hold back her tears so that she could speak.

Persephone nuzzled the top of her head against Lizzy's stomach, and Lizzy knew this was her way of saying goodbye. Suddenly, she turned and leaped off Lizzy's lap and ran towards Ciela.

"Ciela, why can't you and Persephone leave this place?" Lizzy, surprised that she was almost sobbing, stood up and walked toward Ciela as she spoke.

"I must stay and tend the light, Lizzy," Ciela's voice lilted.

"Why can't you bring the light with you, in the lantern?" Lizzy asked, wishing so much this was possible.

"Someday, I will be able to do that. Someday soon, I think. For now, the world is not yet quite ready to see it in its full brightness. For now, it must come more slowly, as each

Changing Girl who visits us takes her little bit of the light back into the world. When enough of the light is in the world, then Persephone and I will be able to return."

"And, yes, Dear, of course you can come back and visit us someday. Remember, you wanted to learn about the archeology of prehistory. And do not forget, each time you have your menstrual period, you will be visiting us!"

Lizzy stood still. The light was now shining more brightly than it ever had. She understood now that it was time to say goodbye. Ciela was moving farther and farther away, walking with a sidewise step so that she could see Lizzy as she moved. Persephone walked slowly beside her. Looking at Ciela from this distance, Lizzy could see only her luminous face, dark shining eyes, and kind smile

"Goodbye, Lizzy," she called out softly.

"Goodbye, Ciela. Thank you for everything."

IX.

Lizzy wiped the tears from her eyes and, when she looked up to wave to Ciela, she was gone. Turning around slowly and picking up her backpack, she took the tiara off her head and put it and the two stalks of wheat she was still holding back into the box.

"I guess I had better get going. By now, I must be late. Mom and Grandma will be worried," she thought to herself as she put her shoes back on and gathered everything up.

Her thoughts continued as she began walking,

"No one is going to believe this. How am going to explain it all?"

Again she noticed that as she walked higher up the ledge, the drawings were fewer and farther between. As she continued walking, she reached a point at which they stopped altogether.

She stopped and thought, "Maybe there are fewer drawing because there have been fewer girls who have learned about becoming Changing Girls."

She had an idea. She reached into her pocket to see if she had saved it. She had! The chalk! She could draw her own Changing Girl picture.

Standing close to the wall, Lizzy began drawing. At first she wasn't even sure what it was she was drawing, and she just let her hand and the chalk move together. Then as it took shape, she saw that she was drawing a picture of herself holding Ciela's gifts and wearing the necklace and Tiara.

It was kind of a stick figure and it even looked kind of funny to her at first. But the more she drew, the more she liked it. And it seemed beautiful in the way that the prehistoric drawings were beautiful. It seemed that because it was so simple, it made it easier for its meaning to show through. Lizzy smiled as she finished her self-portrait.

"I really have to go," she thought, picking up her backpack and the box.

She turned around, paused and then walked right up to the edge of the great ledge. Looking down from this height, the vastness of the space beneath her was breathtaking. The glow of the light seemed more sparkly, and the air smelled sweeter and fresher than ever. The long spiraling ledge seemed infinite.

Breathing in the light and the air and the peace of the Below, Lizzy turned away for the last time and began to leave. Walking slowly at first, then quickening her pace until she was running a little, she felt that she was getting close to the way out. The path got narrower and darker, and she had to slow down again as the cave turned back into a twisting tunnel.

She continued in the little spiral passageway for another few minutes, then up ahead a little way, she could see the fading evening light from outside peeking through an opening. She picked up her pace again, (but was still almost crawling), excited now to be returning to the world above.

When she reached the opening, she had to take off her backpack and first push it and then the gift box through the hole, out into the meadow. Then she poked her head out and took a deep and refreshing breath of air. It was different from the air below, but it felt just as nice to breathe it in. As much as she loved meeting and spending time with Ciela and Persephone, it felt so good to be back in the world of her family and friends and school and . . . everything.

Ciela was right, everything did seem new, and she felt so alive and ready to be her truest self.

Lizzy pulled herself up and out of the cave opening and, reaching over to pick up her backpack, she accidentally kicked the box onto its side and knocked the lid off.

Immediately, she saw the light—the silvery golden shimmering light from Below—glowing from inside of the box! It made a circle of golden light all around her and looked more beautiful than ever shining against the purplish dark of the early evening sky.

"That's what she meant when she said that each Changing Girl brings back a little bit of the light," she thought to herself as she threw her head back and, with her hands clasped behind her head, spun slowly around in the cloud of light that surrounded her.

When she stopped spinning, she was a little dizzy, and her vision was blurred for a few seconds. Once she felt steady again, she found herself looking in the distance at the slightest sliver of a new moon delicately suspended between two hills on the far horizon. The warm, peaceful feeling she had in Ciela's kitchen came over her again as she stood gazing at the silver, serene crescent. It felt just like the moon in her dream— as it shone, it seemed to emanate a fond message to her.

It was different from her dream though, because she wasn't wondering how the moon knew her or what it wanted her to know. It understood her just as Ciela had understood her. It somehow knew that she had changed today; and she knew that it would be her companion throughout the many changing times to come. And she sensed its secrets about change—about how she could be a part of real change in the world, in her world.

Lizzy began walking across the meadow. As she neared the old tree and started back onto the path through the woods, she drew a quick breath and glanced back suddenly, sure that she had seen a little white animal darting across the meadow. There was no trace of it as she surveyed the whole field. It had disappeared into nowhere as quickly as it had come from nowhere.

Turning towards the woods again and walking on down the path, Lizzy smiled inside, thinking that the way home would never be the same again.

About the Author

Jacqueline K. Thomas earned her doctorate in English literature in 2007 from The University of Texas at Austin, having specialized in modernism and nineteenth-century literature, with a focus on anthropology and Ancient Near Eastern and Classical civilizations. She currently resides in Austin, Texas with her husband.

www.ingramcontent.com/pod-product-compliance
Lightning Source LLC
Chambersburg PA
CBHW031536040426
42445CB00010B/559